30 DAY challenge

Embroidery

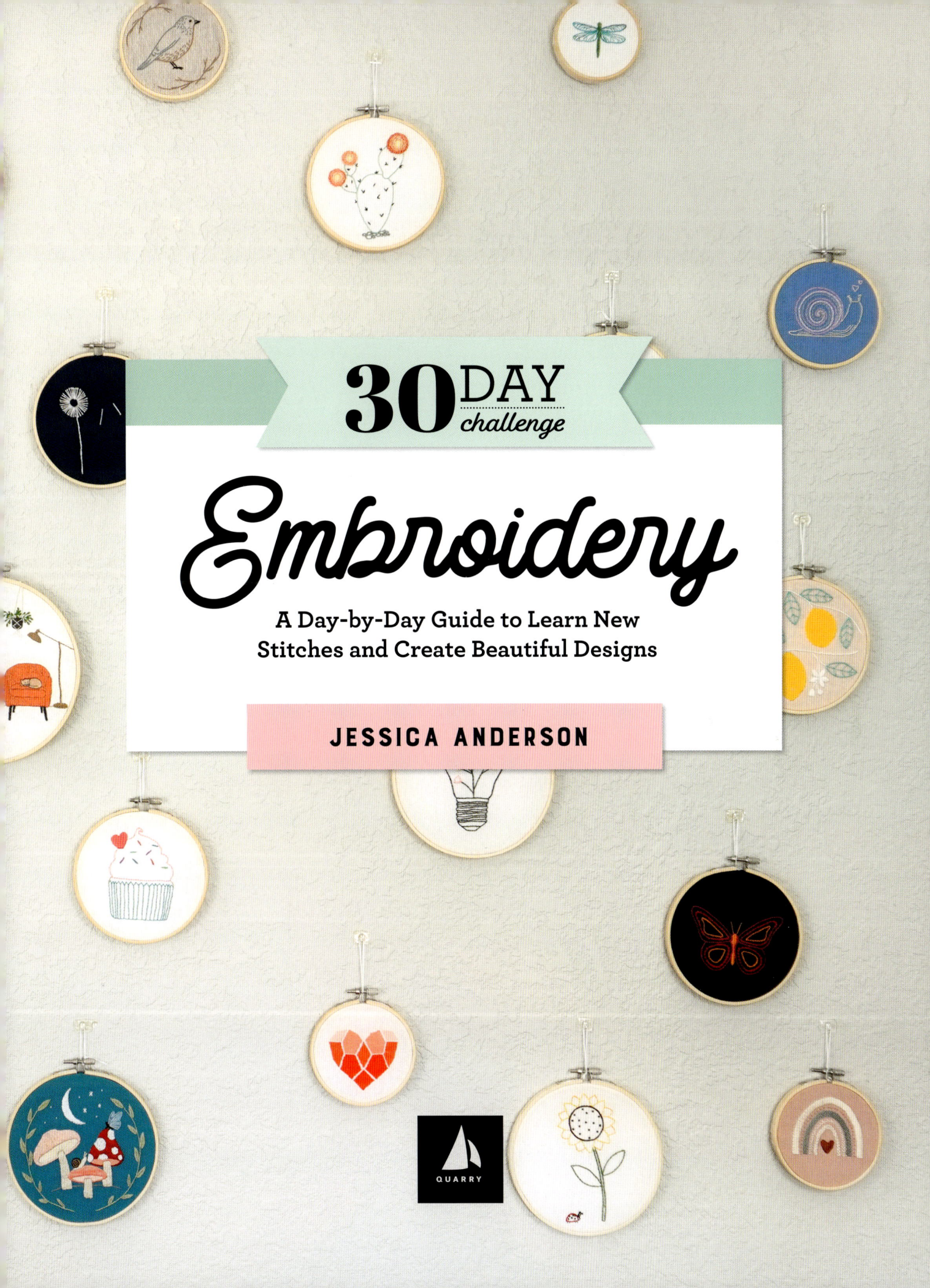

30 DAY challenge

Embroidery

A Day-by-Day Guide to Learn New
Stitches and Create Beautiful Designs

JESSICA ANDERSON

QUARRY

Dedicated to my husband, who lets me follow my dreams, and to my kids, who sometimes eat cereal for dinner.

Quarto.com
© 2024 Quarto Publishing Group USA Inc.
Text, Photos, Illustrations © 2024 Jessica Anderson

First Published in 2024 by Quarry Books, an imprint of The Quarto Group, 100 Cummings Center, Suite 265-D, Beverly, MA 01915, USA.
T (978) 282-9590 F (978) 283-2742

Quarry Books titles are also available at discount for retail, wholesale, promotional, and bulk purchase. For details, contact the Special Sales Manager by email at specialsales@quarto.com or by mail at The Quarto Group, Attn: Special Sales Manager, 100 Cummings Center, Suite 265-D, Beverly, MA 01915, USA.

10 9 8 7 6 5 4 3 2 1

ISBN: 978-0-7603-8491-6

Digital edition published in 2024
eISBN: 978-0-7603-8492-3

Library of Congress Cataloging-in-Publication Data

Names: Anderson, Jessica, 1982- author.
Title: 30 day challenge : embroidery : a day-by-day guide to learn new stitches and create beautiful designs / Jessica Anderson.
Description: Beverly, MA : Quarry Books, 2024. | Series: 30-day craft challenge | Includes index. | Summary: "30 Day Challenge : Embroidery is an easy-to-follow program for beginning stitchers to learn embroidery basics, master new stitches, and create dozens of modern embroidery projects"-- Provided by publisher.
Identifiers: LCCN 2023021710 | ISBN 9780760384916 (trade paperback) | ISBN 9780760384923 (ebook)
Subjects: LCSH: Embroidery--Patterns. | Embroidery--Technique.
Classification: LCC TT771 .A535 2024 | DDC 746.44041--dc23/eng/20230629
LC record available at https://lccn.loc.gov/202
Cover Art, Design and Page Layout: Mattie Wells

Printed in China

Acknowledgments

Thank you to my family for supporting me and making me who I am. I'm so grateful for my mom, Jannet, who taught me to love crafts, and my dad, Mike, who taught me how to work hard. Thanks to my sisters, Jennifer and Jackie, for listening to me drone on about all the things I'm working on, and my brother, Jason, for helping me with technical stuff. Thank you to my husband, Joe, and my kids, Evan, Audrey, Leah, and Austin, who have to put up with all of my crazy ideas. And thank you to my bonus parents, Patti and Greg, for always being so kind and supportive.

Thanks to Kim Adair and Alli Jensen, my hype girls, who convinced me I could write a book *and* have fun doing it. Thank you to Jenna Severin, for helping me stitch several of these designs so I could finish on time. Big thank you to Michelle Bredeson, my editor, for reaching out to me with this book idea and guiding me along the way. Thanks to everyone else at Quarto who worked so hard to make this book come to life.

And finally, thank you to all of my online followers, readers, students, and friends for the encouragement you've given me throughout the years. I love being able to share my creative obsessions with you!

Contents

Project Gallery 8

Introduction 13

chapter 1
Getting Started

Embroidery Supplies 16

Separating Embroidery Floss 20

Securing Threads 21

Managing Traveling Threads 22

Transferring Patterns 23

Setting Up Your Hoops 25

chapter 2
30 Days, 30 Stitches, 30 Projects

Day 1: STRAIGHT STITCH
Geometric Hummingbird 30

Day 2: RUNNING STITCH
Sunshine and Rainbows 32

Day 3: BACK STITCH
Love Letter 34

Day 4: SPLIT STITCH
Floss Bobbin Heartbeat 36

Day 5: LAZY DAISY STITCH
Daisy Bouquet 38

Day 6: CHAIN STITCH
Swirly Snail 40

Day 7: STEM STITCH
Illuminate 42

Day 8: FISHBONE STITCH
Happy Houseplant 44

Day 9: SATIN STITCH
Geometric Heart 46

Day 10: LONG AND SHORT STITCH
Dragonfly 48

Day 11: COUCHING STITCH
Light as a Feather 50

Day 12: FRENCH KNOT
Happy Sunflower 52

Day 13: COLONIAL KNOT
Freshly Picked. 54

Day 14: BULLION KNOT
Just Add Sprinkles 56

Day 15: PISTIL STITCH
Dandelion Wishes. 58

Day 16: PALESTRINA STITCH
Bold Butterfly. 60

Day 17: FLY STITCH
In the Garden 62

Day 18: FEATHER STITCH
Koi Pond. 64

Day 19: HERRINGBONE STITCH
Windy Day. 66

Day 20: BRICK STITCH
Boho Rainbow 68

Day 21: BUTTONHOLE STITCH
Busy Bee Garden. 70

Day 22: SEED STITCH
Birdseed. 72

Day 23: STAR STITCH
Hourglass. 74

Day 24: CHEVRON STITCH
Ombré Pineapple 76

Day 25: BASKETWEAVE STITCH
Lovely Lemons 78

Day 26: THREADED RUNNING STITCH
Fly Away. 80

Day 27: WHIPPED BACK STITCH
Day at the Beach 82

Day 28: WOVEN WHEEL STITCH
Wanderlust 84

Day 29: LOOPED BLANKET STITCH
Cactus Flowers. 86

Day 30: TURKEY STITCH
Beautiful Ballerina. 88

chapter 3

Next Steps

Bonus Challenge Projects 92

Finishing Your Hoops. 98

Ideas for Using Embroidery. . . . 100

Traceable Templates 102

Index 127

Project Gallery

This gallery showcases the 30 main embroidery projects in this book. You can work your way through the projects from first to last or look around the gallery, select the one you want to try, and turn to the relevant page to create your chosen piece. The later projects feature multiple stitches and are a bit more complex, so if you're new to stitching, start with the earlier projects to learn new stitches and get some practice.

Geometric Hummingbird

Page 30

Sunshine and Rainbows

Page 32

Love Letter

Page 34

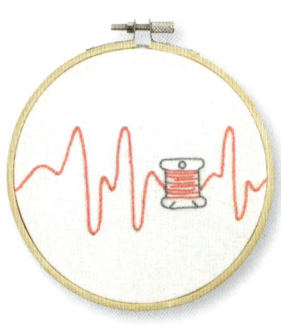

Floss Bobbin Heartbeat

Page 36

Daisy Bouquet

Page 38

Swirly Snail

Page 40

Illuminate

Page 42

Happy Houseplant

Page 44

Geometric Heart

Page 46

Dragonfly

Page 48

Light as a Feather

Page 50

Happy Sunflower

Page 52

Freshly Picked

Page 54

Just Add Sprinkles

Page 56

Dandelion Wishes

Page 58

Bold Butterfly

Page 60

In the Garden

Page 62

Koi Pond

Page 64

Windy Day

Page 66

Boho Rainbow

Page 68

Busy Bee Garden

Page 70

Birdseed

Page 72

Hourglass

Page 74

Ombré Pineapple

Page 76

Lovely Lemons

Page 78

Fly Away

Page 80

Day at the Beach

Page 82

Wanderlust

Page 84

Cactus Flowers

Page 86

Beautiful Ballerina

Page 88

Bonus Projects

These two additional projects combine many types of stitches and will take a bit more time to complete.

Page 93

Page 96

Introduction

When I first learned to embroider, I found learning each stitch individually to be boring and uninspiring. I wanted to jump right into embroidering fun designs, but didn't know where to start. In teaching others to embroider, I noticed some of the same feelings in my students. That's where this book comes in. *30-Day Challenge: Embroidery* not only shows you how to create thirty different stitches, but each one is accompanied by a cute, simple design to practice the stitch. Now you can progressively learn embroidery stitches in a fun way and have some pretty projects to show off afterward. What better motivation to keep practicing? When you're done, you'll be ready to conquer almost any embroidery pattern. In fact, I've even included two challenge embroidery designs at the end. They should really put your skills to the test!

Try to remember, as you're working your way through this book, that your stitches do not need to look perfect. The imperfection is what gives your piece character and makes it look handmade. Most of all, enjoy your relaxing new hobby. It's one I've continued to enjoy for many years (which is saying a lot, since I tend to jump around to new hobbies frequently). I hope you love it as much as I do!

CHAPTER 1

Getting Started

One of the joys of learning embroidery is that the barriers to entry are very low, compared to many other crafts and hobbies. You need just a few supplies and very simple techniques to get started stitching. Once you have your hoop set up, your design transferred to your fabric, and your needle threaded and secured, you will be off and running! In this chapter, you'll learn all of the basics you need to know to set yourself up for success with this relaxing, versatile, and timeless craft.

Embroidery Supplies

There are a few basic supplies you'll need for almost every embroidery project. You don't need to spend a lot of money, which is definitely a plus when trying out a new craft.

FABRIC

For the most part, if you can stick a needle through it, you can embroider on it. Some fabrics, however, are much easier to work with, especially for beginners. Woven, as opposed to knit, fabrics are more stable to stitch. Linen and cotton are the most popular fibers. My favorite fabric to stitch on is a linen/cotton blend called Essex Linen by Robert Kaufman. It has a smooth surface, the needle glides through it easily, and it comes in an array of lovely colors. You can also use 100-percent linen or cotton if those are easier for you to find.

EMBROIDERY FLOSS

Having good-quality embroidery floss is important. The lower-quality brands can tangle easily, break, and may contain dyes that run in the wash. All of the projects in this book are stitched with DMC brand floss, and I have listed the colors I used and their corresponding numbers in parenthesis. Feel free to experiment and try new colors. That's part of the fun! A strand of embroidery floss is actually made up of six separate strands. More on that in the next section.

EMBROIDERY HOOPS

The designs in this book suggest a final hoop size for framing. When I'm stitching, I like to use one size up from that to make sure the hoop doesn't get in the way of my stitches. I recommend using a good-quality wooden hoop when embroidering, then use a less expensive hoop if you want to frame your finished designs.

EMBROIDERY NEEDLES

Embroidery needles come in several different sizes. The size needle you use will be determined by the amount of embroidery floss you're using. A smaller number equals a bigger needle. I recommend the following needle sizes: one strand = size 10 needle, two strands = size 9 needle, three strands = size 8 needle, six strands = size 3 needle. I also like to have a bullion, or milliner's, needle for stitching bullion knots.

Mind Your Needles!

If you've ever had to crawl around looking for a needle you dropped or, worse, stepped on one, I don't have to tell you that dropping a needle is no fun. I use a magnetic needle minder to hold my needle while I'm cutting a new piece of thread or taking a break from my stitching. No more missing needles!

SCISSORS

Small embroidery scissors are best, but any scissors will do in a pinch. Just make sure they're nice and sharp to get a clean cut on your embroidery floss.

NEEDLE THREADER

If you find yourself struggling to thread a needle, try out a needle threader. The ones made with wire break easily, so try to find one with a metal hook instead. Automatic needle threaders are also very nice for threading anything less than six strands of embroidery floss on a needle.

TRANSFER SUPPLIES

There are many different methods to transfer an embroidery pattern to your fabric, but for my favorite methods you will need a FriXion pen, a light table (or a sunny window), and water-soluble stabilizer, such as Sulky Fabri-Solvy (the self-adhesive kind). (See page 23 for instructions on transferring templates.)

Separating Embroidery Floss

Embroidery floss is made up of six separate strands of thread. You can separate those strands to make your stitches thinner. Each pattern will instruct you on how many strands to use for each stitch. To prepare your thread for stitching, follow these steps.

Step 1. Pull out a piece of embroidery floss about the length of your hand to your shoulder. Cut the thread. Separate out the number of strands you need.

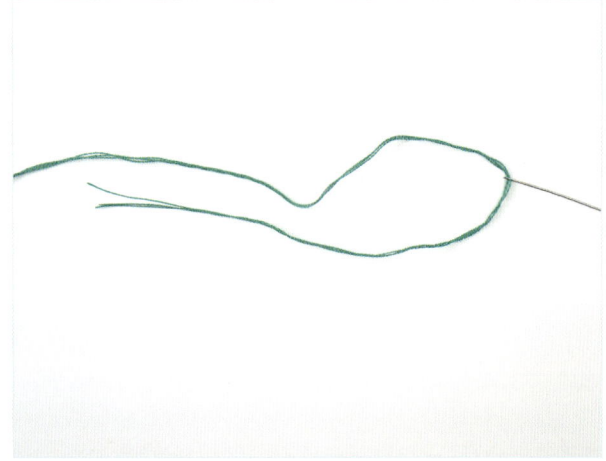

Step 2. Thread the appropriately sized needle (see Embroidery Needles on page 18) with one end of the embroidery floss and pull it through a few inches.

How Many Strands Should You Use?

In this book, each project has a key that indicates how many strands I used for each stitch. When you're creating your own designs, or if you want to modify a design, use more strands for lines and elements you want to really stand out, and fewer strands for the ones you want to recede a bit.

For this geometric hummingbird (page 30), I wanted the stitching to be very consistent so I worked all of the lines in three strands of straight stitch.

Securing Threads

Every time you start stitching with a new length of thread, you'll need to keep it from slipping through the fabric, then stop it from coming loose when you're done.

STARTING

Every new section of stitching starts with securing the embroidery floss in the back. There are some fancy ways to do this, but beginners should just start by tying a knot on the long end of the thread. When you bring your needle up through the back of the fabric, the knot will catch, and you're ready to start stitching.

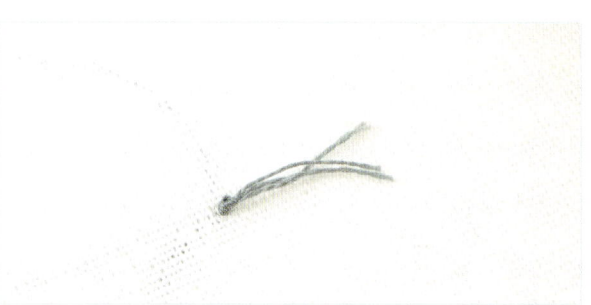

A simple knot secures the thread so it won't pull through.

STOPPING

When you're done with a color, or your thread is about to run out, it's time to secure the thread in the back again.

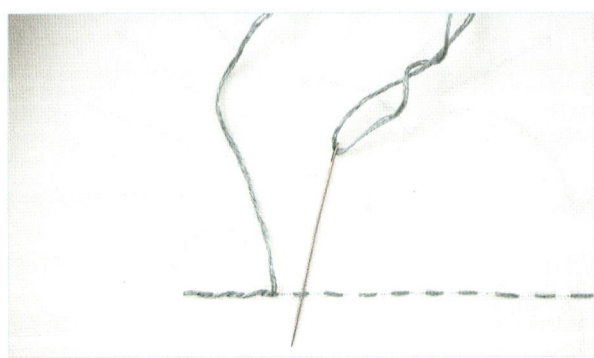

Make sure you stopped stitching with a few inches of thread left. Run your needle under the backs of some of the other stitches a few times, then snip off the excess thread.

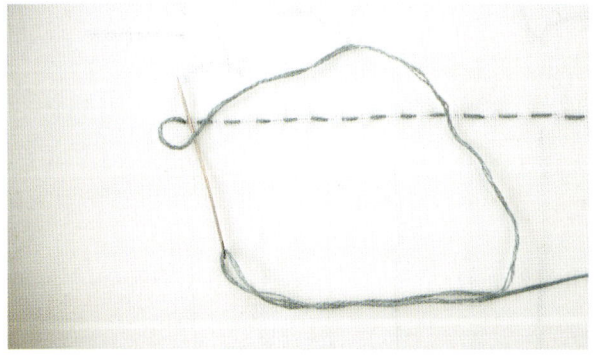

If you don't have a lot of stitches on the back, or you feel like it's not secure enough, you can also use the back of another stitch to tie a knot. Run the needle under the back of a stitch, leaving a loop. Put the needle through the loop and pull to tighten it. Repeat to make the knot secure.

Managing Traveling Threads

When you're working on one area of your piece and you need to start on another area, make sure any thread going across the back (the traveling thread) is not showing through. This is especially important when stitching on light-colored fabrics. The best way to avoid this is to secure your thread and restart in the new area.

You can see how the traveling thread is visible when it's not obscured by thread in the front.

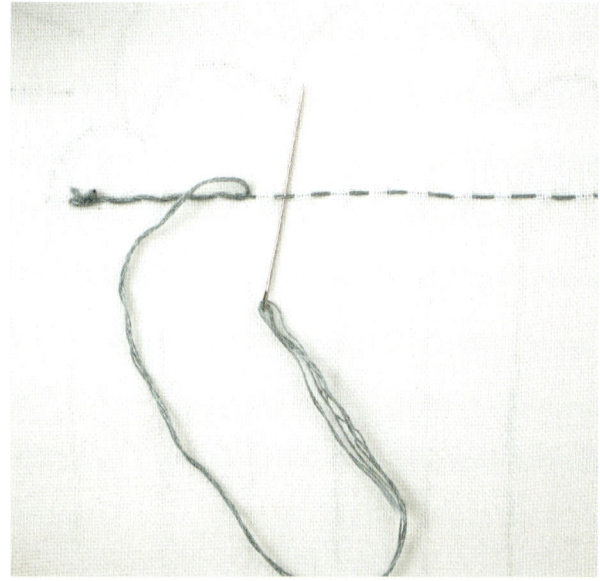

You can also hide your stitches by moving along the backs of other stitches, running your needle under them as you go.

Transferring Patterns

At the end of the book, you'll find black-and-white templates to trace each embroidery pattern. There are many different methods you can use to transfer the patterns to your fabric. We'll go over two of them here.

LIGHT FABRIC

My favorite method for transferring a pattern to light-colored fabric uses a FriXion pen and a light table (or sunny window).

Step 1. Place the template on a light table or tape it to a sunny window. Center a piece of fabric over the template.

Step 2. Trace the pattern onto the fabric using a FriXion pen. Be sure to draw only on areas that will be covered with stitches. The markings mostly disappear with heat but can still be faintly seen when not covered by stitches. They can also reappear in very cold temperatures. When you're done stitching, use a blow-dryer or iron over any visible marks to make them disappear.

DARK FABRIC

This method for dark or patterned fabric can also be used for light fabric if you find you like it better. You'll need Sulky Fabri-Solvy stabilizer (the self-adhesive kind) and your FriXion pen.

Step 1. Cut a piece of stabilizer slightly larger than the template. Place the stabilizer on top of the template with the soft side up. Trace the pattern onto the stabilizer using a FriXion pen. (You can technically use any pen, but I like to use FriXion just in case the ink runs.)

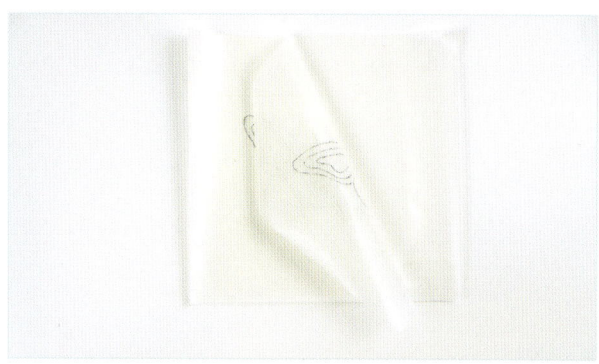

Step 2. Peel the paper backing off the stabilizer.

Step 3. Apply the stabilizer to your fabric like a sticker, then place the fabric in a hoop as usual (see page 25).

Step 4. Embroider through the stabilizer and fabric.

Step 5. When you're done, soak your project in cold water while agitating it to remove all of the stabilizer. Gently squeeze the excess water out of the edges of your fabric, avoiding the embroidery. Lay flat to dry.

Setting Up Your Hoops

Putting your fabric in an embroidery hoop is an essential step to keep it from puckering as you stitch. Here's how it's done:

Step 1. Cut a piece of fabric slightly larger than your hoop. Loosen the screw at the top of your embroidery hoop and separate the inside ring from the outer ring. Place the fabric on top of the inside ring and center it.

Step 2. Line the outer ring up with the inside ring on top of the fabric and press it down. Tighten the screw a little and make sure the fabric is drum tight. (If you tap it with your finger, it should feel tight and make a little noise like a drum.) If it's not tight enough, pull the fabric evenly around the hoop until it tightens. Make sure your transferred image doesn't get distorted. Once your fabric is tight enough, fully tighten the screw at the top of the embroidery hoop.

CHAPTER 2

30 Days, 30 Stitches, 30 Projects

Now that you have your supplies ready and know the basics of transferring your designs, setting up your hoop, and working with embroidery thread, you're ready to jump in and learn some stitches! This chapter includes thirty different common and more unusual embroidery stitches and thirty designs that feature the stitches. You can give yourself a crash course in embroidery by completing one project each day for a month or take your time and go at your own pace. Either way, you will have a lot of fun and make great progress in learning this rewarding craft.

Stitch Glossary

All of the thirty stitches included here are shown and described in this chapter. Step-by-step illustrations show exactly how to create them. Use this handy reference to find stitches you'd like to try (if you don't choose to go in order) or to refer back to stitches you want to use in future projects.

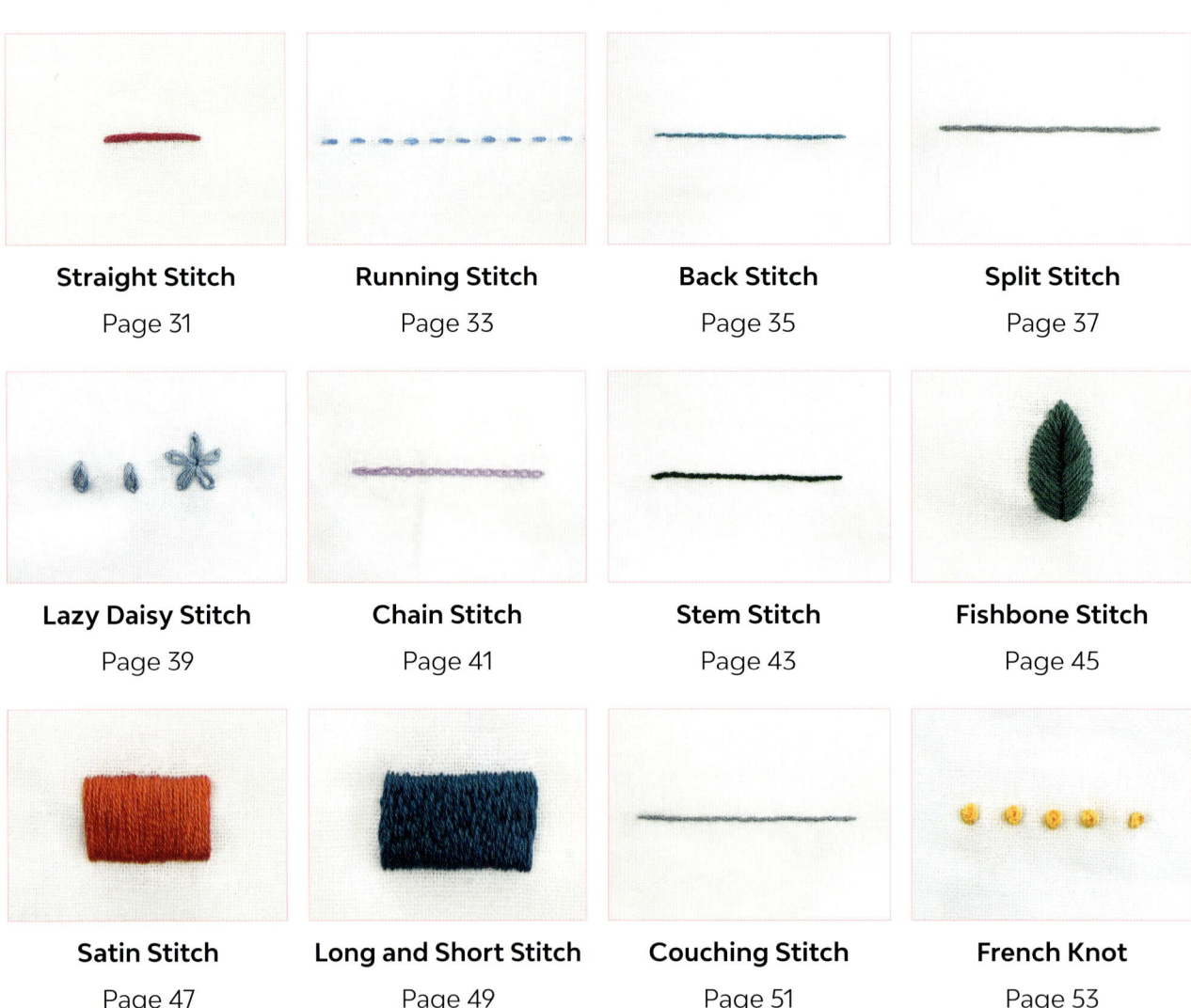

Straight Stitch

Page 31

Running Stitch

Page 33

Back Stitch

Page 35

Split Stitch

Page 37

Lazy Daisy Stitch

Page 39

Chain Stitch

Page 41

Stem Stitch

Page 43

Fishbone Stitch

Page 45

Satin Stitch

Page 47

Long and Short Stitch

Page 49

Couching Stitch

Page 51

French Knot

Page 53

Colonial Knot
Page 55

Bullion Knot
Page 57

Pistil Stitch
Page 59

Palestrina Stitch
Page 61

Fly Stitch
Page 63

Feather Stitch
Page 65

Herringbone Stitch
Page 67

Brick Stitch
Page 69

Buttonhole Stitch
Page 71

Seed Stitch
Page 73

Star Stitch
Page 75

Chevron Stitch
Page 77

Basketweave Stitch
Page 79

Threaded Running Stitch
Page 81

Whipped Back Stitch
Page 83

Woven Wheel Stitch
Page 85

Looped Blanket Stitch
Page 87

Turkey Stitch
Page 89

Geometric Hummingbird

Be extra careful on this one to hide your thread on the back. Travel only along lines that you know will be covered on the front and avoid skipping to different areas. This will keep the back of your thread from showing on the front (see Managing Traveling Threads on page 22).

STRAIGHT STITCH

The straight stitch is just what it sounds like, a single stitch in a straight line. We start with it because it's the most basic of all the stitches and it's used to create several of the more complex stitches.

Bring the needle up at A and down at B.

YOU WILL NEED

White fabric

5-inch (12.5 cm) embroidery hoop

Template (page 103)

EMBROIDERY FLOSS

● pink (3350)

● medium green (701)

● dark green (895)

● lime green (704)

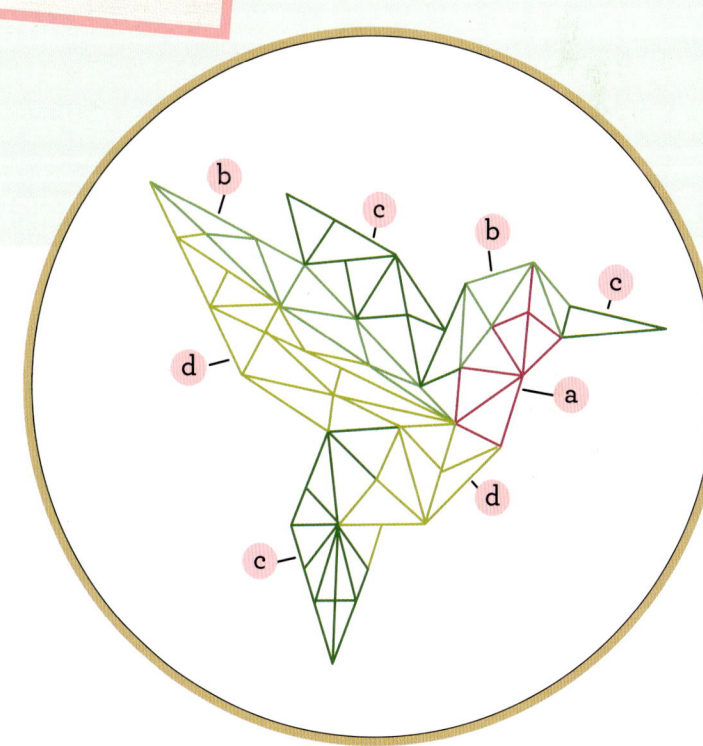

KEY

a: Straight stitch, pink, 3 strands

b: Straight stitch, medium green, 3 strands

c: Straight stitch, dark green, 3 strands

d: Straight stitch, lime green, 3 strands

Sunshine and Rainbows

With this project, have fun with the rainbow section and make the stitches different lengths if you want. It adds interest to the design and will help you learn how to control the lengths of your stitches.

RUNNING STITCH

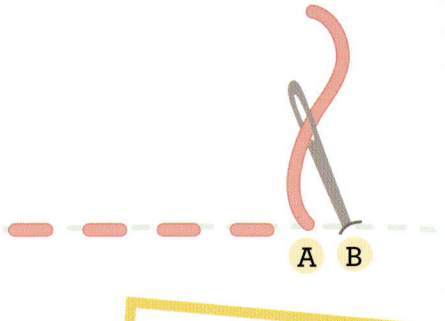

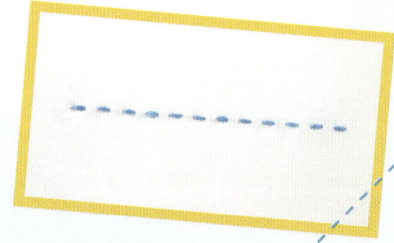

The running stitch is what you might imagine when you think of hand stitching. It creates a dotted line that is super simple but adds a nice, handmade look to any project. Generally, when doing the running stitch, you want all the stitches to be about the same length.

Step 1. Bring needle up at A and down at B.

Continue. Repeat at even intervals.

YOU WILL NEED

White fabric

6-inch (15 cm) embroidery hoop

Template (page 103)

EMBROIDERY FLOSS

- gray (169)
- dark yellow (676)
- red (3722)
- orange (977)
- yellow (3078)
- green (913)
- blue (799)
- purple (340)
- violet (316)

KEY

a: Running stitch, gray, 3 strands

b: Running stitch, dark yellow, 3 strands

c: Running stitch, red, 3 strands

d: Running stitch, orange, 3 strands

e: Running stitch, yellow, 3 strands

f: Running stitch, green, 3 strands

g: Running stitch, blue, 3 strands

h: Running stitch, purple, 3 strands

i: Running stitch, violet, 3 strands

Love Letter

As with the running stitch, you want to shorten your stitches on the curves. This is especially important on the tight curves of the letters. Letters can be tricky because your brain expects perfection and wants them to look a certain way. Take your time, use small stitches, and try not to be a perfectionist!

BACK STITCH

The back stitch is the easiest way to create a solid line when stitching. It starts out like a running stitch, but instead of going forward to continue the stitch, you go backward. Hence the name back stitch.

Step 1. Bring the needle up at A and down at B.

Step 2. Bring the needle up at C and down at A. Repeat at even intervals.

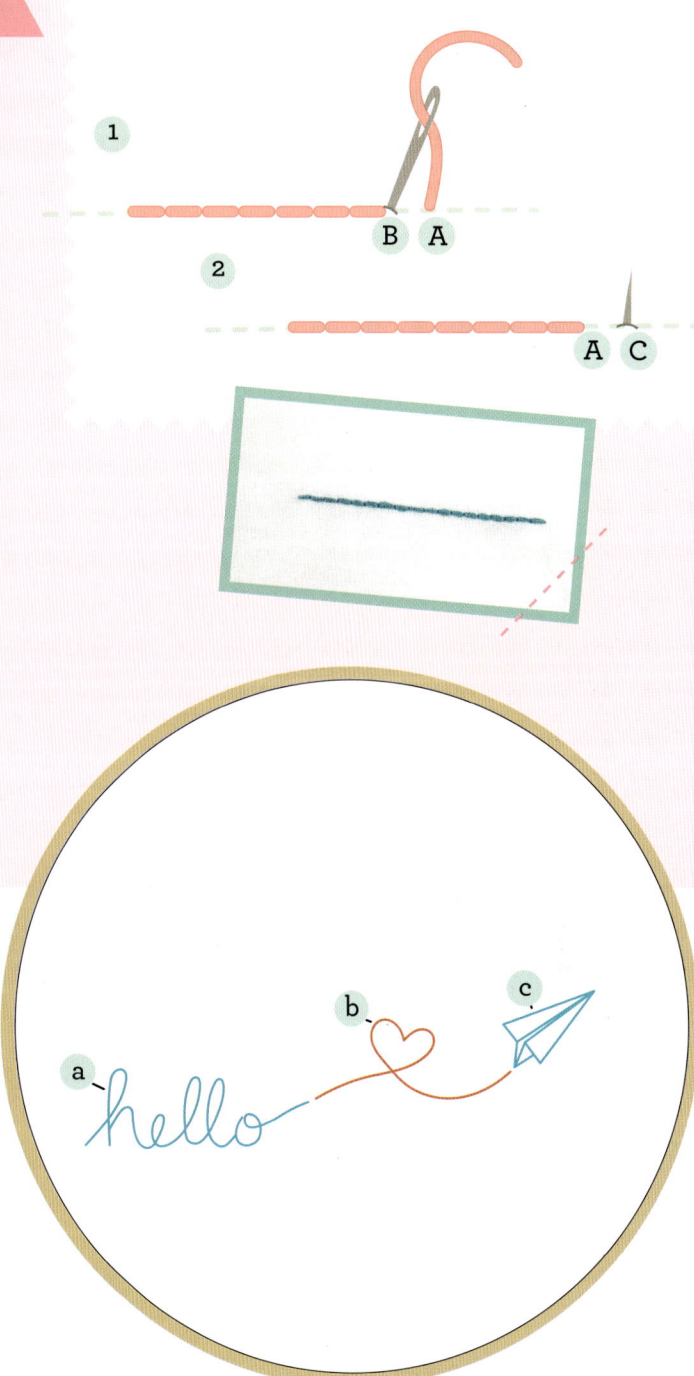

YOU WILL NEED

White fabric

5-inch (12.5 cm) embroidery hoop

Template (page 107)

EMBROIDERY FLOSS

● blue (3810)

● red (350)

KEY

a: Back stitch, blue, 3 strands

b: Running stitch, red, 3 strands

c: Straight stitch, blue, 2 strands

Floss Bobbin Heartbeat

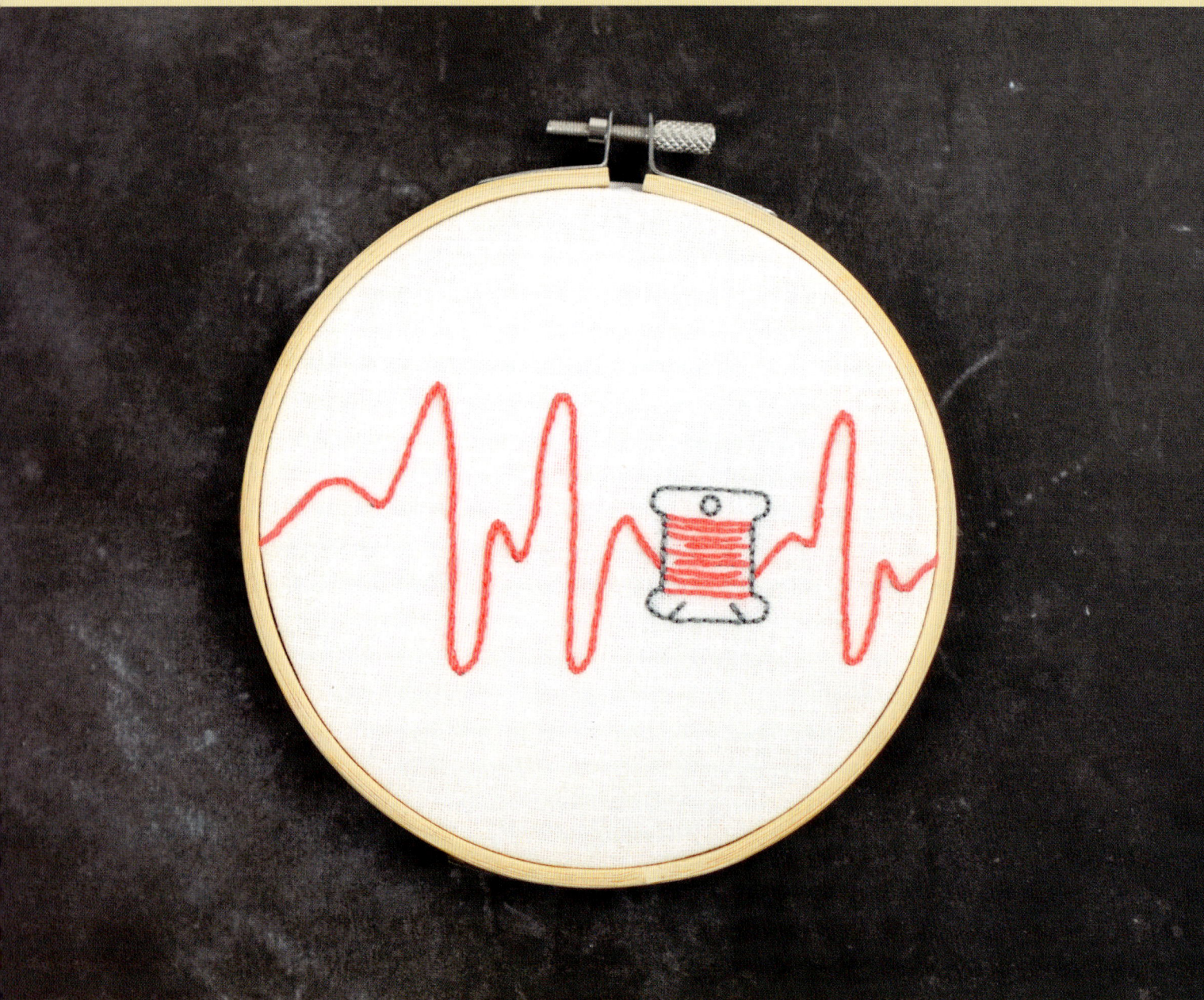

After completing this book, I hope you have a sense that embroidery is part of who you are. Maybe after a while, you'll feel like it's part of what keeps your heart beating. Okay, not really, but the image is still fun. This one should be fairly easy to stitch. As always, just keep the stitches short on those curves!

SPLIT STITCH

The split stitch is another great way to create a line. It has a different texture and is sometimes easier to work around curves than the back stitch. It is created by bringing your needle up through the middle of the previous stitch, splitting it, which is why it's called a split stitch.

Step 1. Bring the needle up at A in the middle of the previous stitch, splitting the thread. Bring the needle down at B.

Step 2. Continue by bringing the needle up at C and repeating at even intervals.

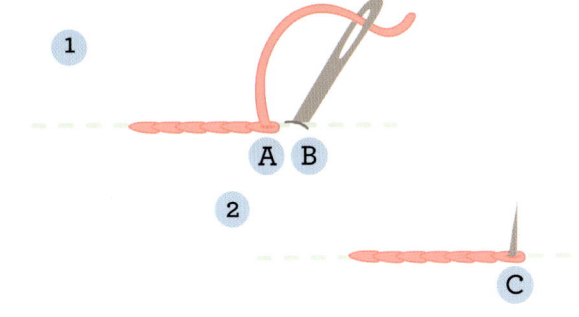

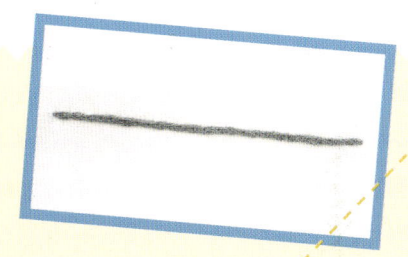

YOU WILL NEED

White fabric

5-inch (12.5 cm) embroidery hoop

Template (page 111)

EMBROIDERY FLOSS

● pink (893)

● gray (169)

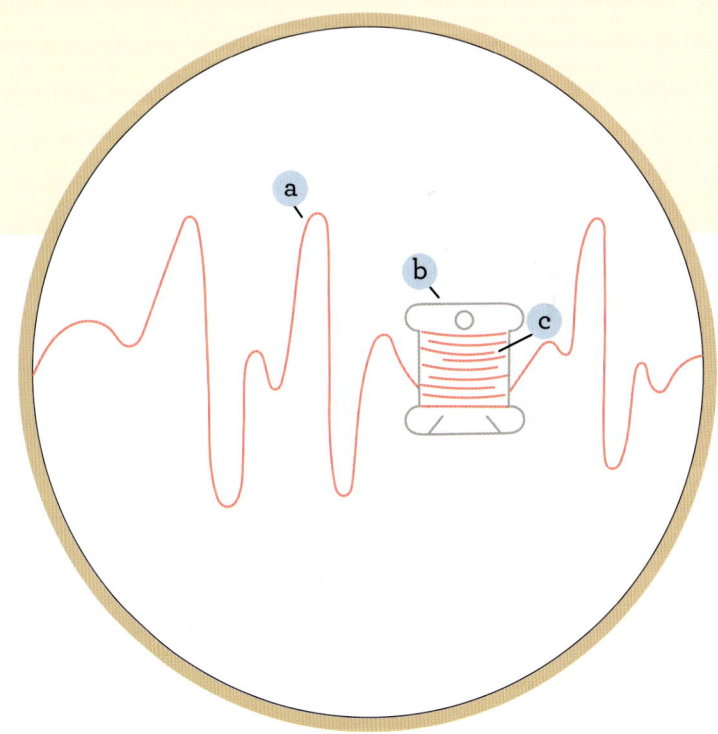

KEY

a: Split stitch, pink, 3 strands

b: Back stitch, gray, 3 strands

c: Split stitch, pink, 2 strands

Daisy Bouquet

In this pattern you'll use the lazy daisy stitch to make traditional, five-petal daisy flowers, and you'll also use it in a different formation to make butterflies. I used a natural linen-colored fabric, but as with any of the patterns, feel free to change up the colors.

LAZY DAISY STITCH

The lazy daisy stitch is a very simple way to create a flower. If you make one of the petals by itself, it creates a teardrop shape, which is also known as a detached chain stitch. Use this stitch for flowers, raindrops, small leaves, and more.

Step 1. Bring the needle up at A and back down at A, leaving a loop.

Step 2. Bring the needle up at B, through the loop, and pull gently to tighten the loop. Keep the loop loose to retain the teardrop shape.

Step 3. Bring the needle over the end of the loop and down at C to create a very small stitch to hold down the end of the loop.

Step 4. To make a lazy daisy flower, repeat the above steps to create five more petals in a circle, all starting at A.

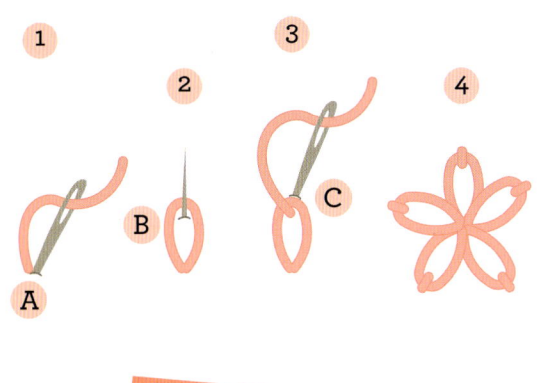

YOU WILL NEED

Natural linen-colored fabric

6-inch (15 cm) embroidery hoop

Template (page 109)

EMBROIDERY FLOSS

- dark gray (3768)
- blue (932)
- pink (758)
- purple (3042)
- green (3053)

KEY

a: Back stitch, dark gray, 3 strands

b: Lazy daisy stitch, blue, 2 strands

c: Straight stitch, blue, 3 strands

d: Lazy daisy stitch, pink, 2 strands

e: Lazy daisy stitch, purple, 2 strands

f: Split stitch, green, 2 strands

Swirly Snail

I just love the colors on this cute little snail! The chain stitch adds a beautiful texture to his shell and is so fun to make. The curves on the hearts and the snail's antennae are very tight, so make super tiny stitches in those spots.

CHAIN STITCH

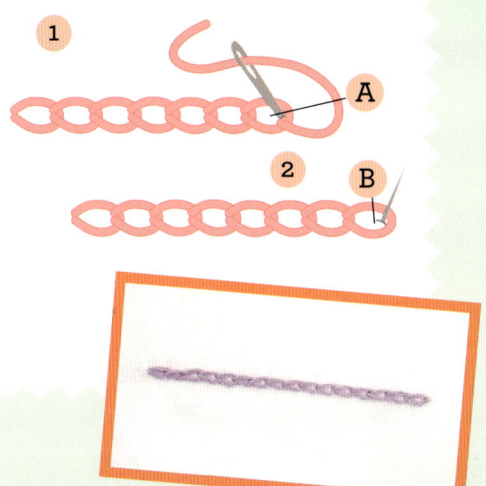

The chain stitch makes—you guessed it—a chain. You'll notice that it's basically like making a bunch of lazy daisy stitches chained together. It's a nice stitch to use when you want to add a bit of texture to a line, or it can even be used to fill in an area. In fact, we'll be doing that in a later pattern.

Step 1. Bring the needle up at A and back down at A, leaving a loop.

Step 2. Bring the needle up at B, through the loop, and pull gently to tighten the loop. Keep the loop loose to retain the teardrop shape. Bring the needle back down at B and repeat the process above, making a chain of loops in a line. To finish the chain, make a small stitch over the last loop, just like you do in a lazy daisy stitch.

YOU WILL NEED

Periwinkle fabric

4-inch (10 cm) embroidery hoop

Template (page 111)

EMBROIDERY FLOSS

- purple (554)
- pink (3713)
- blue (932)
- yellow (3823)

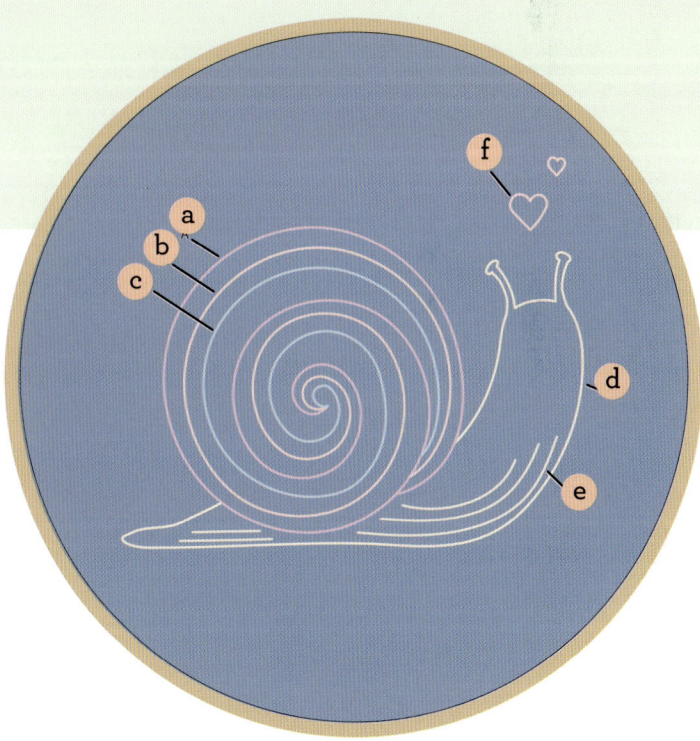

KEY

a: Chain stitch, purple, 2 strands

b: Chain stitch, pink, 2 strands

c: Chain stitch, blue, 2 strands

d: Stem stitch, yellow, 2 strands

e: Back stitch, yellow, 2 strands

f: Split stitch, pink, 2 strands

Illuminate

I love this floral lightbulb pattern! It's something I sketched up a long time ago and hadn't gotten around to embroidering yet. If you want to challenge yourself a bit, you could add a quote about light. This is another stitch that you'll want to shorten on tight curves, although this pattern doesn't have too many.

STEM STITCH

The stem stitch is my favorite stitch for creating a line. It works beautifully on curved lines and is perfect for plant stems.

Step 1. For the first stitch only, bring the needle up at A and down at B; do not pull tight yet.

Step 2. Bring the needle up at C, pulling the needle up/above the stitch to tighten.

Step 3. For all following stitches, bring the needle down at D and up at B, pulling the needle up/above the stitch created. Repeat at even intervals, continuing to pull the needle up on the same side of the line every time.

YOU WILL NEED

White fabric

6-inch (15 cm) embroidery hoop

Template (page 105)

EMBROIDERY FLOSS

- ● black (310)
- ● red (351)
- ● pink (3354)
- ● yellow (3047)
- ● green (319)

KEY

a: Stem stitch, black, 2 strands

b: Back stitch, black, 2 strands

c: Split stitch, red, 2 strands

d: Lazy daisy stitch, pink, 2 strands

e: Back stitch, pink, 2 strands

f: Lazy daisy stitch, yellow, 2 strands

g: Stem stitch, green, 2 strands

Happy Houseplant

This little houseplant will give you plenty of fishbone-stitch practice. The pattern calls for just two strands on the leaves, which makes them really smooth. If you want more textured leaves, you can try using three or even six strands. For the trunk of the plant, you will be doing parallel rows of stem stitch to fill it with color.

TIP

With filling stitches, stitch just barely outside the line of the shape, rather than directly on the line. That will help the edges look more defined and consistent.

FISHBONE STITCH

1

A
B

2

C E
D F

3

D

This stitch is named the fishbone stitch because the pattern it creates resembles that of fish bones (are you seeing a pattern with these stitch names?). It's my favorite stitch for filling in leaves. It takes a bit of practice to make a perfect leaf, but you'll get the hang of it quickly.

Step 1. Bring the needle up at A and down at B.

Step 2. Bring the needle up at C and down at D (slightly below B). Bring the needle up at E and down at F (slightly below D).

Step 3. Continue filling in the shape, alternating left and right sides.

YOU WILL NEED

White fabric

3-inch (7.5 cm) embroidery hoop

Template (page 123)

EMBROIDERY FLOSS

- green (501)
- black (310)
- brown (840)

KEY

a: Fishbone stitch, green, 2 strands

b: Split stitch, black, 2 strands

c: Straight stitch, black, 2 strands

d: Fill with rows of stem stitch, brown, 2 strands

e: Stem stitch, brown, 2 strands

Geometric Heart

The fading colors on this geometric heart pattern are so pretty and make it look like a gemstone. Filling in areas on a pattern can take a long time, so I tried to keep this one small. You can make a copy of the pattern and make it even smaller if it still seems like it's taking too long. Or enlarge it if you want an extra challenge!

SATIN STITCH

The satin stitch is the most common stitch used to fill an area with color (thread). It's basically a bunch of straight stitches, super close together, that fill a shape. This one can be a little tricky at first, but always looks better with practice. Just like with the fishbone stitch, I find it's best to aim for bringing my needle up and down just outside the line of the shape. It can be helpful to draw directional lines on the inside of the shape for you to follow.

Bring the needle up at A and down at B. Bring the needle up at C, close to A. Repeat, making straight stitches parallel to each other until shape is filled.

YOU WILL NEED

White fabric

4-inch (10 cm) embroidery pattern

Template (page 109)

EMBROIDERY FLOSS

● red (350)

● dark pink (351)

● medium pink (352)

● light pink (353)

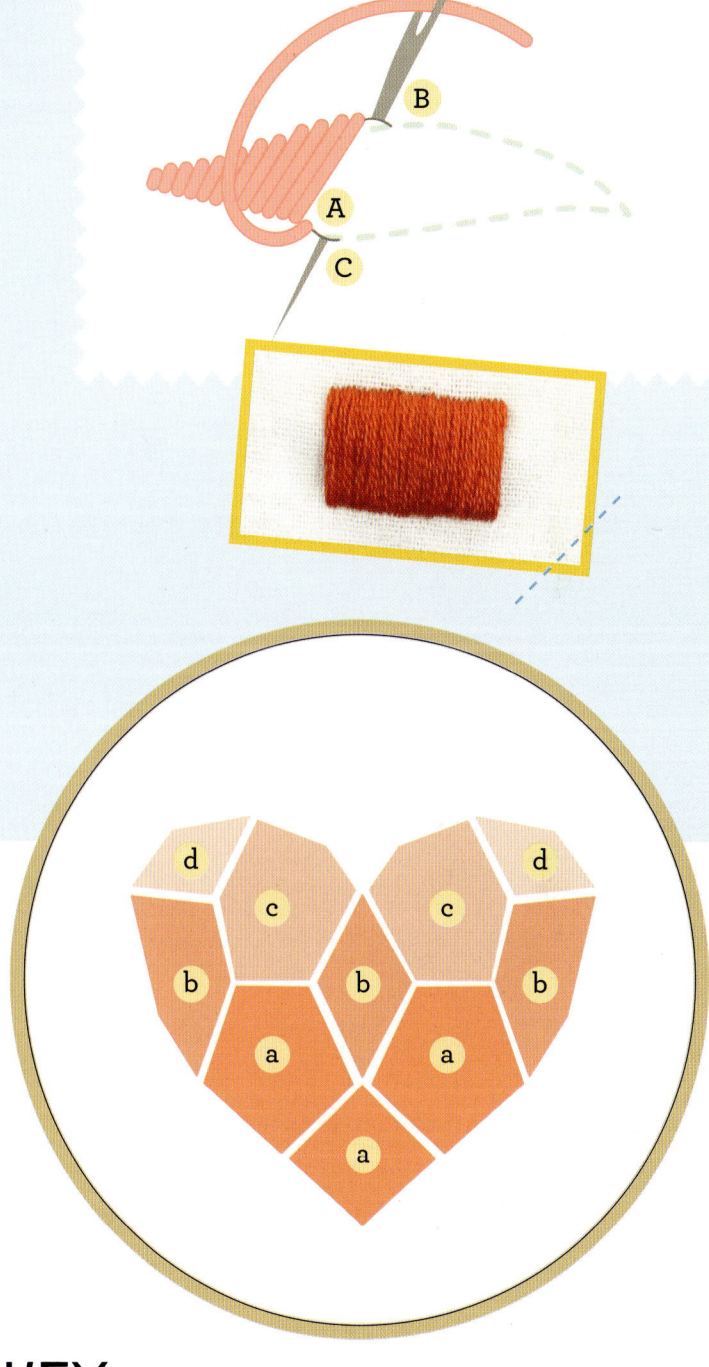

KEY

a: Satin stitch, red, 2 strands

b: Satin stitch, dark pink, 2 strands

c: Satin stitch, medium pink, 2 strands

d: Satin stitch, light pink, 2 strands

Dragonfly

This pattern calls for a single strand of embroidery floss, which gives you a very smooth long and short stitch. It's a bit tricky—and that's when good-quality embroidery floss is really important—but you can do it!

TIP

You use just a single strand for some of the split stitch, since the veins on the wings are so small.

LONG AND SHORT STITCH

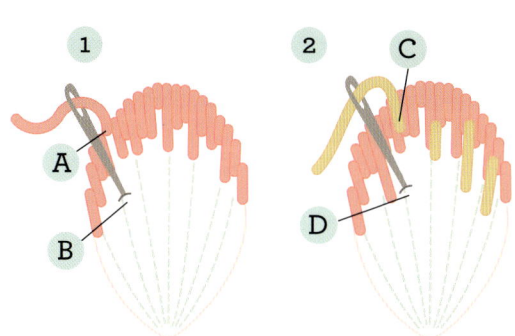

If a shape is too large, and you try to fill it with a satin stitch, the stitches won't stay flat. That's when the long and short stitch comes in handy. It's best for filling in areas that are too large or irregularly shaped for the satin stitch. There are a few different variations of the long and short stitch. The one we are using here is frequently used in a technique called silk shading/ thread painting, where you switch from one color to anther and blend them to create shading effects. That's a more advanced technique, so we're going to stick with just one color here.

Step 1. Start on one side of the shape and make small, random-length stitches along the edge, bringing the needle up at A and down at B.

Step 2. Start a new row of stitches, bringing the needle up at C (between the previous row of stitches) and down at D. Continue with multiple rows of stitches until the shape is filled.

YOU WILL NEED

White fabric

3-inch (7.5 cm) embroidery hoop

Template (page 121)

EMBROIDERY FLOSS

● green (4045)

● blue (4025)

KEY

a: Long and short stitch, green, 1 strand

b: Split stitch, blue, 2 strands

c: Split stitch, blue, 1 strand

Light as a Feather

This feather is the perfect opportunity to practice the couching stitch. I used a color-changing embroidery floss again, but this one is a little more subtle. It has some light grays and white in it, which stands out against the teal background fabric.

COUCHING STITCH

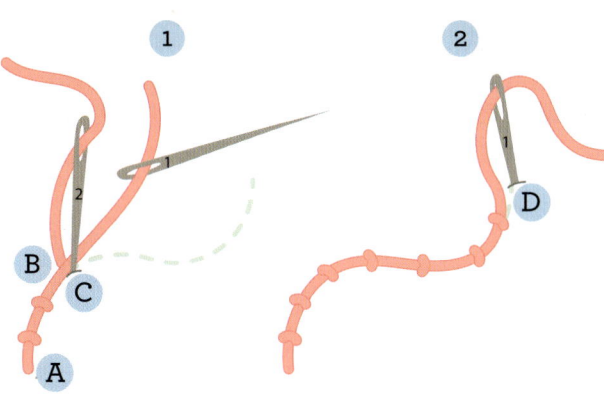

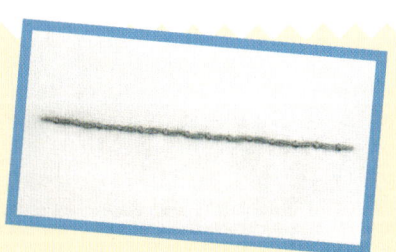

The couching stitch is interesting because you actually thread two needles and have two working threads going at once. One thread lays across the fabric, while the other one makes small stitches over it, down the line, to secure it in place. Make both strings the same color for a consistent line or use two different colors for a different effect.

Step 1. Bring needle 1 up at A and lay thread along the line. Bring needle 2 up at B and down at C, making small stitches at even intervals over the laying thread.

Step 2. Bring needle 1 down at D at the end of the line.

YOU WILL NEED

Teal fabric

5-inch (12.5 cm) embroidery hoop

Template (page 105)

EMBROIDERY FLOSS

 gray (4015)

KEY

a: Fill with rows of back stitch, gray, 2 strands

b: Couching stitch, gray, 3 strands

Happy Sunflower

You'll get to practice French knots on the sunflower and the little ladybug in this pattern. Notice that on the flower, the knots are just a little larger since they're made with three strands versus the two strands on the ladybug. For an extra challenge, you can try filling the leaves with a fishbone stitch instead of just outlining them.

FRENCH KNOT

The French knot creates a small knot on the surface of your project. It's one of my favorite stitches because it adds that special, homemade touch. They can be a little hard at first, but with practice will become second nature. Make them by themselves or in clusters to fill in an area with texture.

Step 1. Bring the needle up at A. With the needle pointed away from A, wrap the thread around twice.

Step 2. Hold the thread with your non-dominant hand while turning the needle toward the fabric, and bring the needle down at B (just slightly away from A). Continue to loosely hold the thread while bringing the needle down, and let go just before the knot is created.

YOU WILL NEED

White fabric

6-inch (15 cm) embroidery hoop

Template (page 103)

EMBROIDERY FLOSS

- dark brown (938)
- yellow (726)
- orange (728)
- green (3346)
- red (817)
- black (310)

KEY

a: Split stitch, dark brown, 3 strands

b: French knot, dark brown, 3 strands

c: Back stitch, yellow, 3 strands

d: Back stitch, orange, 3 strands

e: Stem stitch, green, 3 strands

f: Split stitch, red, 2 strands

g: Split stitch, black, 2 strands

h: French knot, black, 2 strands

i: Straight stitch, black, 2 strands

Freshly Picked

Now you get to see how it looks to fill an area with knots. This is a great texture for flower centers, and I've even used it for making curly hair on a person. Coneflowers have a very textured center, so I knew filling them with knots would be perfect. If you're short on time, you can outline the flower petals instead of filling them with satin stitch.

COLONIAL KNOT

If the French knot gave you trouble, don't fret. Many people find colonial knots a bit easier to execute. You can use them anywhere you would use a French knot since they look basically the same. You'll start by making a backward "C" shape with your thread, so I like to think "C" for colonial when I remember how to make it.

Step 1. Bring the needle up at A. Make a backward "C" shape with your thread and put the end of the needle through it, pointing away from you.

Step 2. Turn the needle so it points to the left. Wrap the thread up, over, and around the needle to make a sideways figure-eight shape.

Step 3. Gently pull the thread to tighten the knot around needle, and bring the needle down at B (just slightly away from A). Continue to loosely hold the thread while bringing the needle down, and let go just before the knot is created.

YOU WILL NEED

White fabric

6-inch (15 cm) embroidery hoop

Template (page 111)

EMBROIDERY FLOSS

- gray (169)
- blue (519)
- green (3346)
- pink (3727)
- dark red (3857)

KEY

a: Split stitch, gray, 3 strands

b: Split stitch, blue, 3 strands

c: Back stitch, green, 2 strands

d: Satin stitch, pink, 3 strands

e: Fill with colonial knots, dark red, 3 strands

Just Add Sprinkles

This cute cupcake is just begging to be stitched for someone's birthday! The bullion-knot sprinkles really stand out, and the pink satin-stitched heart is so cute. Feel free to play around with the colors and really make this pattern your own.

BULLION KNOT

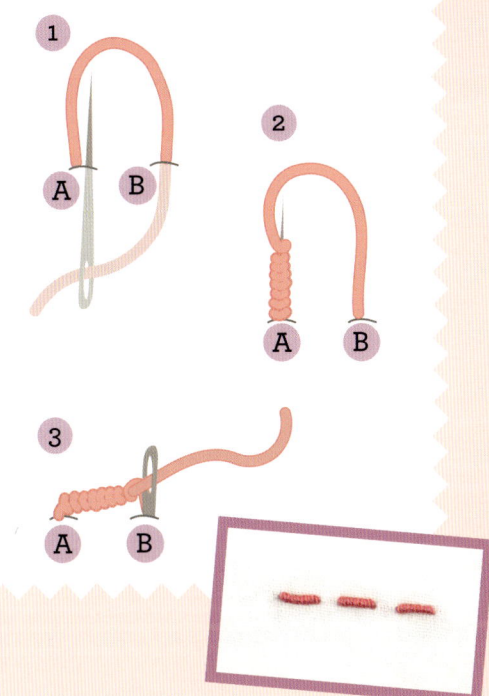

The bullion knot makes a long, skinny knot. It helps if you use a milliner's needle or bullion knot needle to make them.

Step 1. Bring the needle up at A, down at B, and back up at A, leaving a large loop on top of the fabric.

Step 2. Tightly wrap the thread coming out of A around the end of the needle several times until the wrapping is the same length as the space from A to B. Loosely hold the wrapping between your thumb and index finger and pull the needle through.

Step 3. Keep wrapping close to A and bring the needle down at B to complete the knot.

YOU WILL NEED

White fabric

5-inch (12.5 cm) embroidery hoop

Template (page 105)

EMBROIDERY FLOSS

● blue (3810)

● light pink (3354)

● brown (3864)

● hot pink (335)

● purple (553)

● green (913)

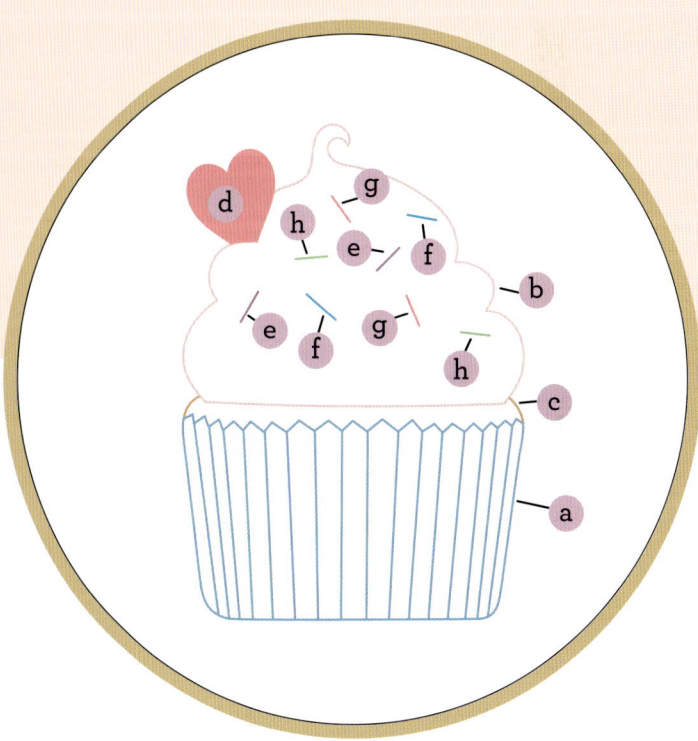

KEY

a: Back stitch, blue, 2 strands

b: Stem stitch, light pink, 2 strands

c: Split stitch, brown, 2 strands

d: Satin stitch, hot pink, 2 strands

e: Bullion knot, purple, 2 strands

f: Bullion knot, blue, 2 strands

g: Bullion knot, hot pink, 2 strands

h: Bullion knot, green, 2 strands

Dandelion Wishes

As a kid, I couldn't pass a dandelion without picking it and making a wish. My children now do the same, and I can't help but smile when looking at this pattern. The pistil stitch is perfect for making the little dandelion seeds. If you want a little more of a challenge, you could add the word "wish" or a quote about dandelions on it.

PISTIL STITCH

This stitch is perfect for making flower pistils and bug antennae. It's just a line with a knot on the end. In fact, it's made just like a French knot, but instead of bringing the needle down right next to the first hole, you insert it farther away to create the line.

Step 1. Bring the needle up at A. With the needle pointed away from A, wrap the thread around twice.

Step 2. Hold the thread with your non-dominant hand while turning needle and bring the needle down at B. Continue to loosely hold the thread while bringing the needle down, and let go just before the knot is created.

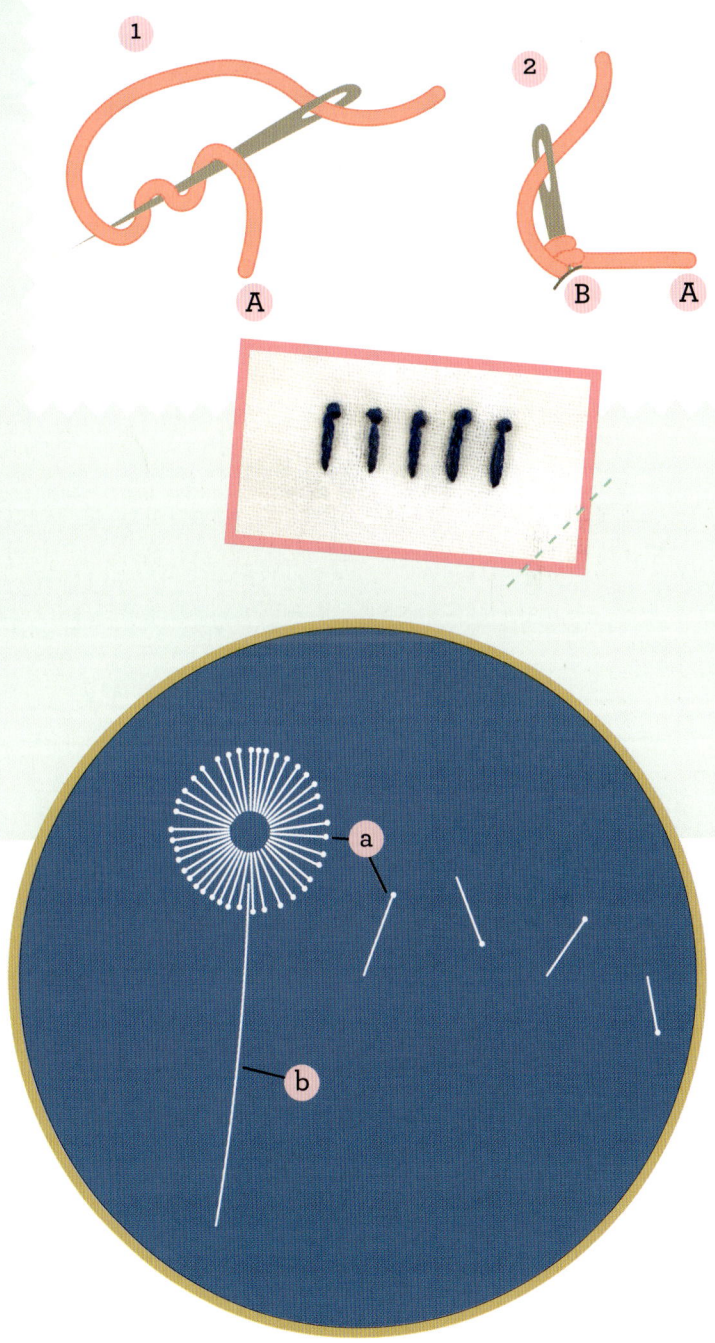

YOU WILL NEED

5-inch (12.5 cm) embroidery hoop

Dark blue fabric

Template (page 115)

EMBROIDERY FLOSS

○ white (BLANC)

KEY

a: Pistil stitch, white, 2 strands
b: Stem stitch, white, 2 strands

Bold Butterfly

This butterfly pattern features the Palestrina stitch along with several other stitches. Feel free to choose your own favorites, or follow the pattern. You can't go wrong.

PALESTRINA STITCH

The palestrina stitch creates a line of knots that form a visually interesting texture. It might seem a little tricky at first, but once you get the hang of it, it's really fun to do. Place the knots close together or far apart for a different look.

Step 1. Bring the needle up at A. Bring it down at B (just above the line) and up again at C (just below the line).

Step 2. Slide the needle under the stitch from the top and pull it to the left.

Step 3. Slide the needle under the top right corner of the first stitch. Bring the needle through the loop (on top of the thread) and pull to the right. Repeat at even intervals along the line.

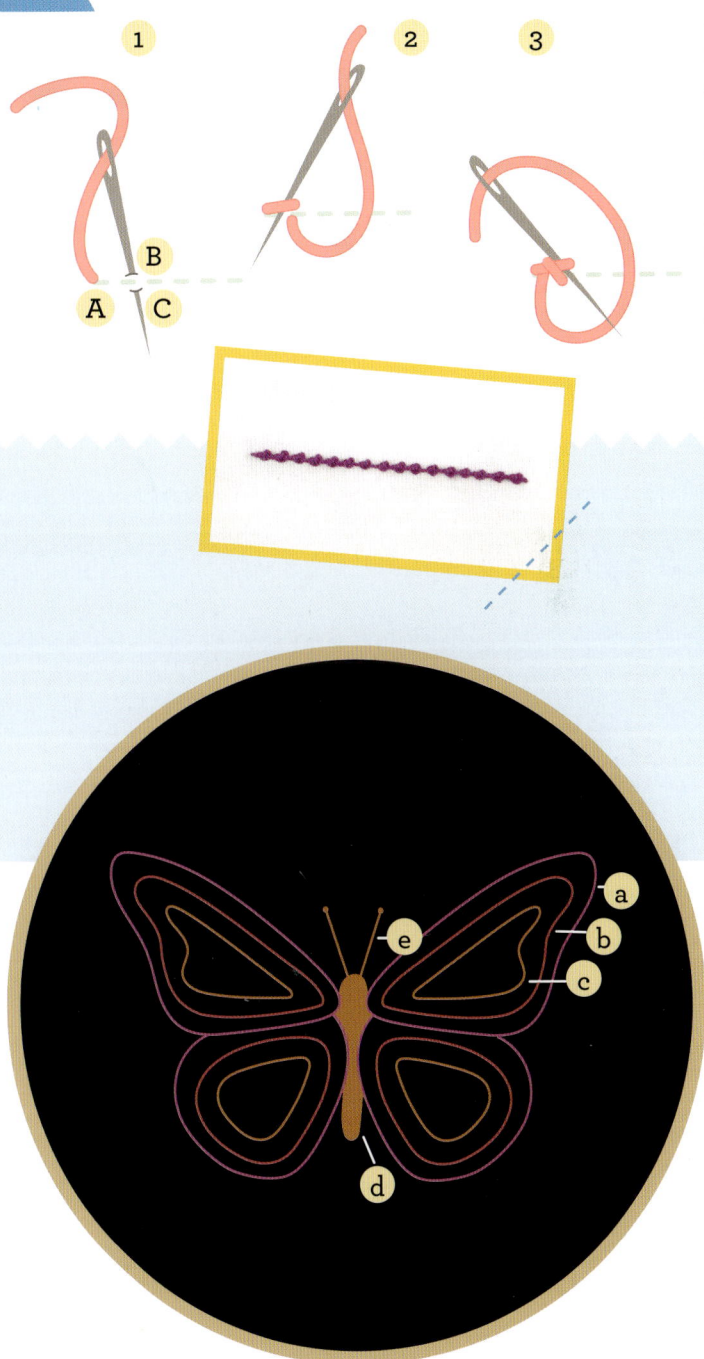

YOU WILL NEED

Black fabric

5-inch (12.5 cm) embroidery hoop

Template (page 105)

EMBROIDERY FLOSS

● pink (718)

● red (3831)

● orange (3776)

KEY

a: Stem stitch, pink, 3 strands

b: Palestrina stitch, red, 3 strands

c: Split stitch, orange, 3 strands

d: Satin stitch, orange, 3 strands

e: Pistil stitch, orange, 3 strands

In the Garden

The image of this little girl in the garden with a giant flower popped into my head as soon as I thought of a fly stitch pattern. The girl uses mostly a single strand of floss and has lots of tiny details. If she's too hard to get right, you can leave her out, or stitch something like a watering can instead.

FLY STITCH

The fly stitch can be used to add a decorative border or make a flower stem like the pattern here. You can also make a tiny stitch (similar to a lazy daisy) to tack down the shape if you don't want the long stem.

Step 1. Bring the needle up at A and down at B, leaving a loop on top of the fabric. Bring the needle up at C, at the bottom of the loop, and pull tight to make a "V" shape.

Step 2. Bring needle down at D.

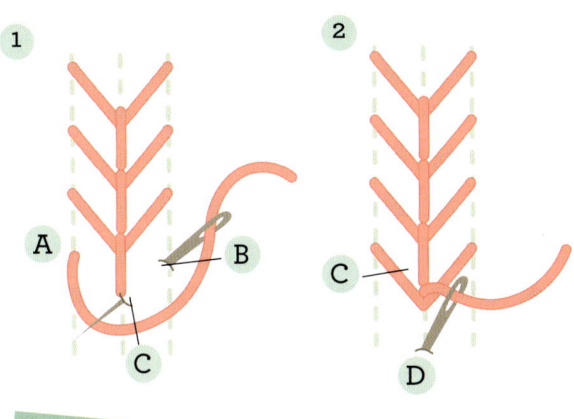

YOU WILL NEED

White fabric

6-inch (15 cm) embroidery hoop

Template (page 113)

EMBROIDERY FLOSS

- ● green (319)
- ● light blue (519)
- ● yellow (726)
- ● dark gray (3799)
- ● red (3831)
- ● light gray (169)
- ● brown (898)
- ● blue (3810)
- ● black (310)

KEY

a: Fly stitch, green, 2 strands

b: Lazy daisy stitch, light blue, 2 strands

c: Satin stitch, yellow, 2 strands

d: Split stitch, dark gray, 1 strand

e: Straight stitch, dark gray, 1 strand

f: Split stitch, red, 2 strands

g: Split stitch, light gray, 2 strands

h: Split stitch, brown, 1 strand

i: Back stitch, blue, 2 strands

j: Straight stitch, blue, 2 strands

k: Split stitch, black, 2 strands

Koi Pond

This koi fish will give you a little bit of practice with the feather stitch on its scales. They start larger, near the head of the fish, and get smaller as they near the tail. I used color-changing thread on the water for a pretty effect. If you're running short on time or patience, you can always outline the cherry blossom flowers instead of filling them in.

FEATHER STITCH

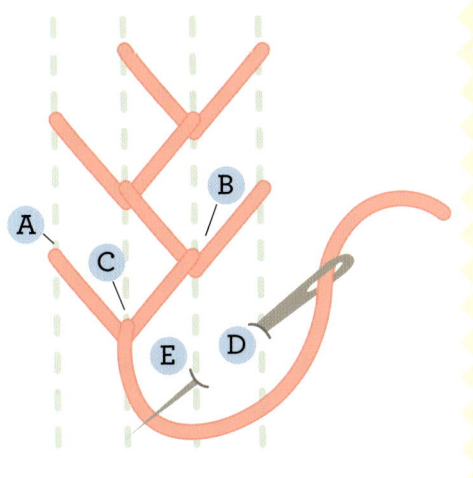

The feather stitch is another pretty decorative stitch. It looks similar to the fly stitch, but it's more like a chain of connected "V" shapes, without the center stem like the fly stitch has.

Step 1. Bring the needle up at A and down at B, leaving a loop on top of the fabric. Bring the needle up at C, at the bottom of the loop, and pull tight to make a "V" shape.

Step 2. Bring the needle down at D, leaving a loop on top of the fabric (just like step 1). Bring the needle up at E, at the bottom of the loop, and pull tight to make a "V" shape. Repeat these steps to continue down the line.

YOU WILL NEED

White fabric

4-inch (10 cm) embroidery hoop

Template (page 113)

EMBROIDERY FLOSS

● orange (3853)

● blue (4025)

● pink (3354)

KEY

a: Stem stitch, orange, 2 strands

b: Feather stitch, orange, 2 strands

c: Straight stitch, orange, 6 strands

d: Split stitch, blue, 3 strands

e: Satin stitch, pink, 3 strands

Windy Day

This colorful pinwheel is a fun one to stitch up. The herringbone stitch really adds a nice texture and design to the pinwheel. Change the colors to your favorite ones to make it even more special to stitch.

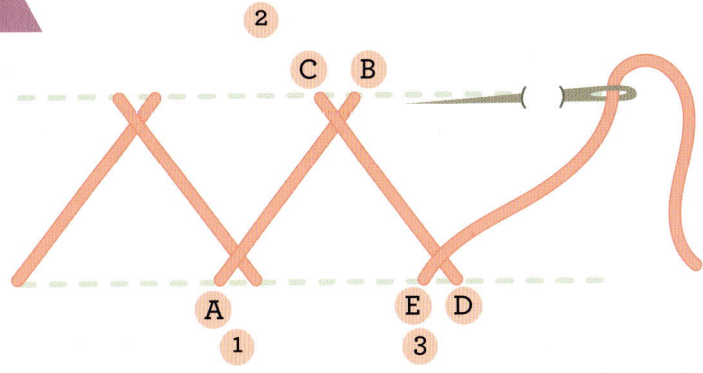

HERRINGBONE STITCH

The herringbone stitch is also a decorative stitch that looks great on borders or hems. It's pretty easy to execute, since you're just making straight stitches in a specific formation.

Step 1. Bring the needle up at A and down at B.

Step 2. Bring the needle up at C and down at D.

Step 3. Repeat steps 1 and 2, starting at E.

YOU WILL NEED

White fabric

6-inch (15 cm) embroidery hoop

Template (page 119)

EMBROIDERY FLOSS

- gray (169)
- red (351)
- purple (553)
- blue (3810)
- green (703)
- light blue (519)
- yellow (3078)

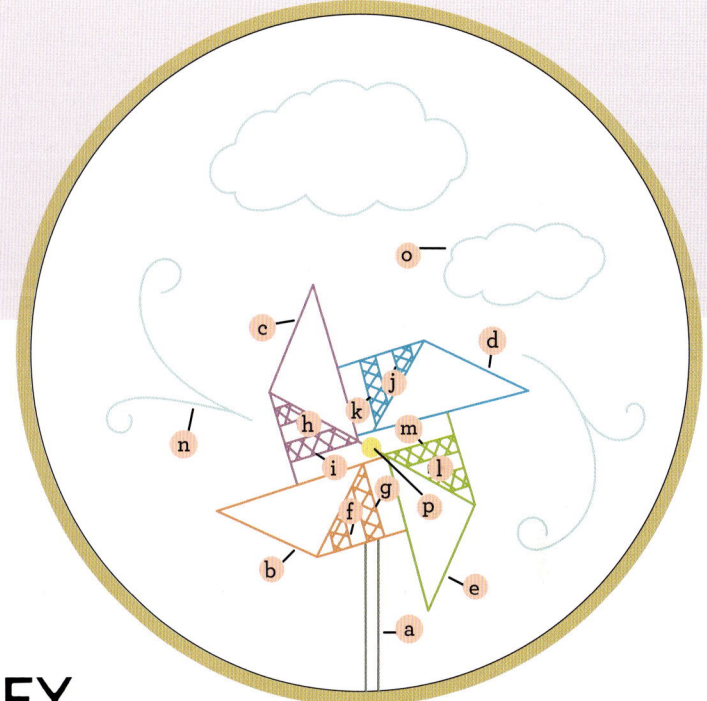

KEY

a: Back stitch, gray, 3 strands

b: Split stitch, red, 2 strands

c: Split stitch, purple, 2 strands

d: Split stitch, blue, 2 strands

e: Split stitch, green, 2 strands

f: Back stitch, red, 2 strands

g: Herringbone stitch, red, 2 strands

h: Back stitch, purple, 2 strands

i: Herringbone stitch, purple, 2 strands

j: Back stitch, blue, 2 strands

k: Herringbone stitch, blue, 2 strands

l: Back stitch, green, 2 strands

m: Herringbone stitch, green, 2 strands

n: Stem stitch, light blue, 3 strands

o: Split stitch, light blue, 3 strands

p: Satin stitch, yellow, 2 strands

Boho Rainbow

This boho rainbow would be so adorable in a nursery or child's room. In fact, I created a larger version of this pattern with a baby name on it for a gift. The textures that the different stitches create really add to the beauty and interest of this design.

BRICK STITCH

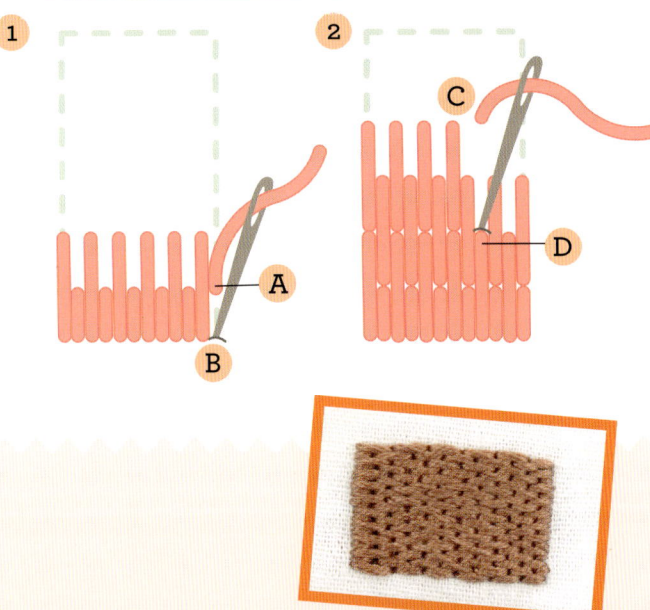

The brick stitch is another form of the long and short stitch that we did on Day 10. The reason I include both is because the brick stitch has a much more uniform texture. The stitches are done at even intervals and resemble the pattern of bricks. It's great for filling in shapes, and I really like using it for filling in lettering.

Step 1. Make alternating long and short stitches along one side of the shape, bringing the needle up at A and down at B. Long stitches should be twice the length of the short stitches.

Step 2. Fill in the rest of the shape with rows of long stitches to create a brick pattern. Bring the needle up at C and down at D.

YOU WILL NEED

Pink fabric

4-inch (10 cm) embroidery hoop

Template (page 111)

EMBROIDERY FLOSS

○ off-white (712)

● pink (407)

● gray (169)

● red (632)

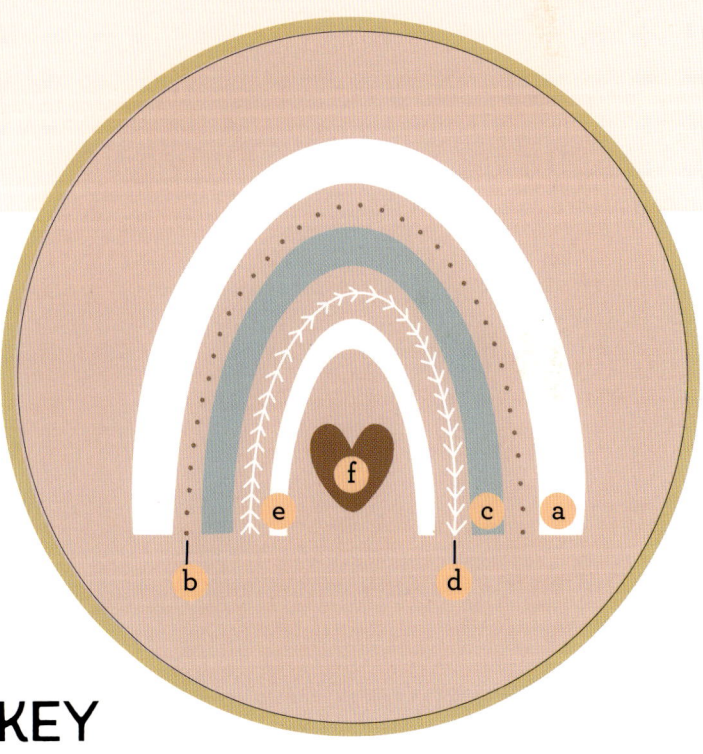

KEY

a: Satin stitch, off-white, 3 strands

b: French knot, pink, 2 strands

c: Brick stitch, gray, 3 strands

d: Fly stitch, off-white, 2 strands

e: 2 rows of chain stitch in opposite directions, off-white, 3 strands

f: Satin stitch, red, 2 strands

Busy Bee Garden

Make the simpler circular buttonhole flowers before attempting the larger three-petal flowers. You'll notice in the stitch diagram that you put the needle back down in the same center hole (B) each time. For the larger flowers, you'll change things up a bit and bring the needle down around the yellow center of the flower instead. If you want to make this pattern a bit simpler, you can just outline the satin stitch parts and/or omit some of the flowers.

BUTTONHOLE STITCH

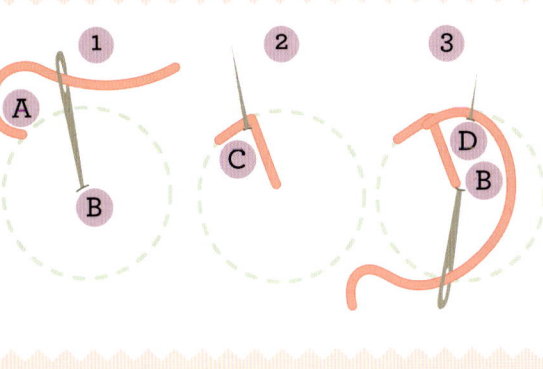

If you've ever done a blanket stitch, this is very similar, the main difference being that it's done in a circular formation. You can make a wagon-wheel looking circle, or more abstract designs that also have curves, like the big flowers in the pattern here.

Step 1. Bring the needle up at A and down at B. Do not pull tight yet.

Step 2. Bring the needle up at C, pulling up to make the previous stitch into a number "7" shape.

Step 3. Repeat by bringing the needle down at B and up at D.

YOU WILL NEED

Light blue fabric

5-inch (12.5 cm) embroidery hoop

Template (page 117)

EMBROIDERY FLOSS

- ● pink (3354)
- ● yellow (3078)
- ● mauve (316)
- ● purple (340)
- ● red (3722)
- ● black (310)
- ● green (913)

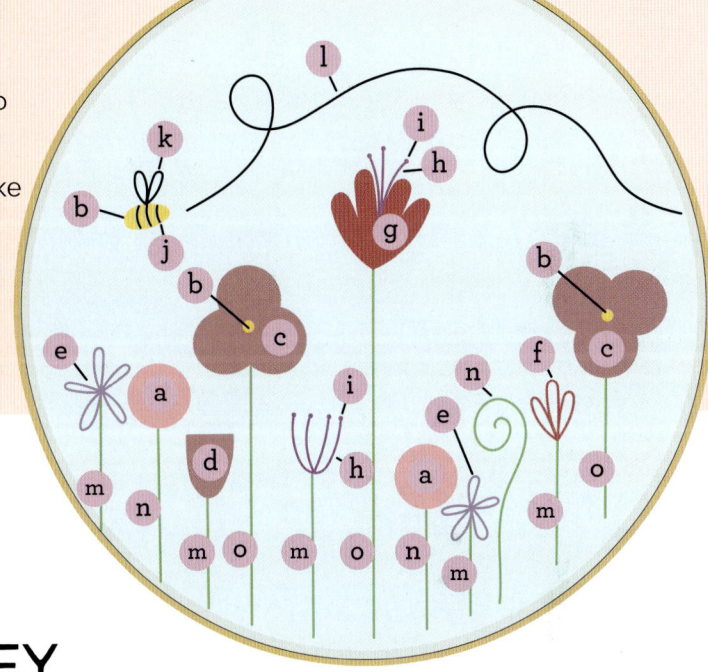

KEY

a: Buttonhole stitch, pink, 2 strands

b: Satin stitch, yellow, 2 strands

c: Buttonhole stitch, mauve, 2 strands

d: Satin stitch (uneven at top), mauve, 3 strands

e: Lazy daisy stitch, purple, 2 strands

f: Lazy daisy stitch, red, 2 strands

g: Satin stitch, red, 2 strands

h: Back stitch, purple, 3 strands

i: French knot, purple, 3 strands

j: Back stitch, black, 2 strands

k: Lazy daisy stitch, black, 2 strands

l: Running stitch, black, 2 strands

m: Split stitch, green, 3 strands

n: Stem stitch, green, 3 strands

o: Back stitch, green, 3 strands

Birdseed

I love the way the seed stitch adds just a little bit of texture and color to this sweet bird pattern without having to fill it in completely. The little white dot on his eye is a very tiny straight stitch—just enough to add a bit of white.

SEED STITCH

The seed stitch looks just like what it's called: a bunch of scattered seeds. It's basically a bunch of small, straight stitches going in random directions to fill in an area. Place them closer together to fill the area completely, or stitch them farther apart for a scattered filling.

Bring the needle up at A and down at B to create a small stitch. Repeat at random angles to fill an area.

YOU WILL NEED

Natural linen-colored fabric

4-inch (10 cm) embroidery hoop

Template (page 115)

EMBROIDERY FLOSS

 blue (931)

 brown (840)

⬤ black (310)

◯ white (BLANC)

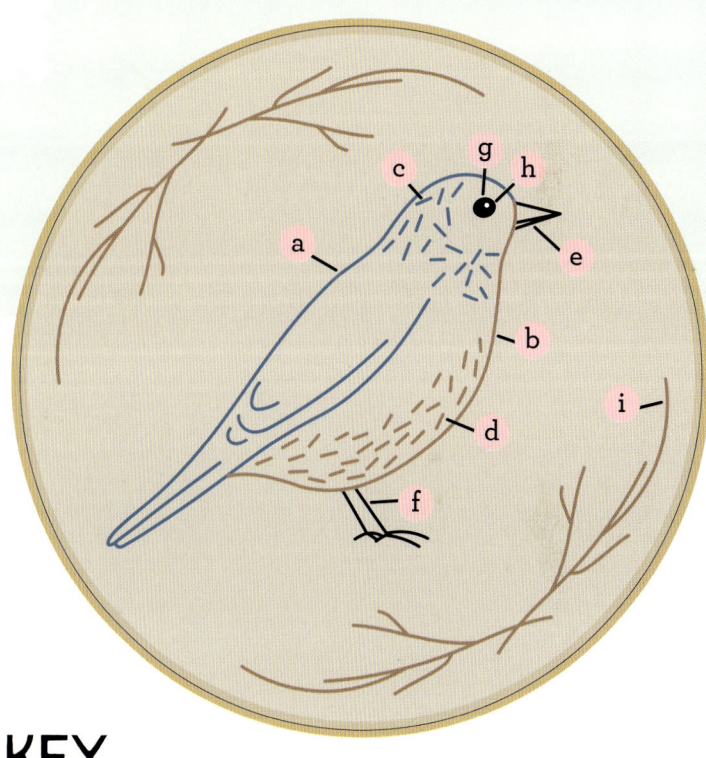

KEY

a: Split stitch, blue, 2 strands

b: Split stitch, brown, 2 strands

c: Seed stitch, blue, 2 strands

d: Seed stitch, brown, 2 strands

e: Straight stitch, black, 2 strands

f: Split stitch, black, 2 strands

g: Satin stitch, black, 2 strands

h: Straight stitch, white, 3 strands

i: Stem stitch, brown, 2 strands

Hourglass

Every time I see an hourglass in a store, I have to turn it over. Something about watching the sand is so relaxing. Mix this pattern up a little and stitch the stars with two different colors of thread each instead of a single color.

STAR STITCH

This is a cute stitch that makes a little twinkly star shape. Make the whole star a single color or make the small "X" in the center a different color for a pretty effect.

Step 1. Bring the needle up at A, down at B, up at C, and down at D to make a cross shape. Bring the needle up at E, down at F, up at G, and down at H to make an "X" shape over the cross.

Step 2. Bring the needle up at I, down at J, up at K, and down at L to make a small "X" over the center of the stitch.

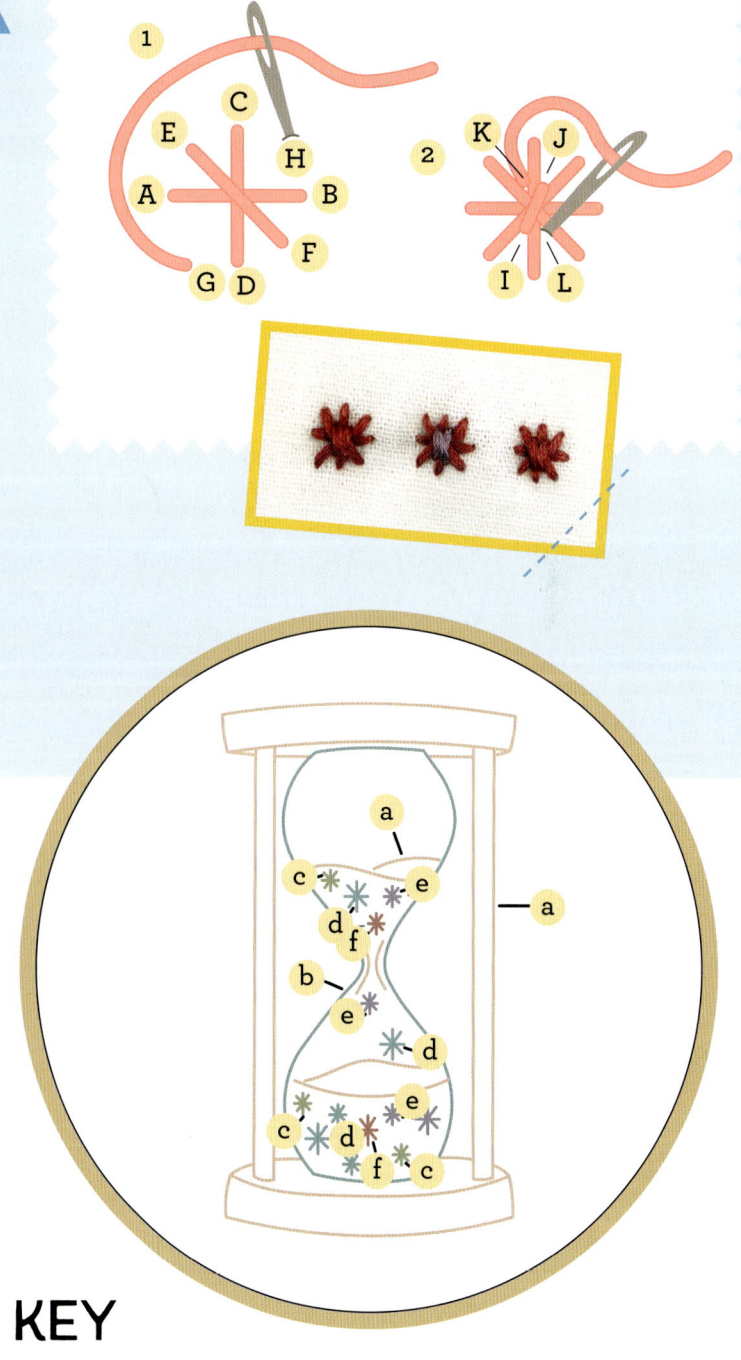

YOU WILL NEED

White fabric

5-inch (12.5 cm) embroidery pattern

Template (page 107)

EMBROIDERY FLOSS

- brown (840)
- blue (3810)
- green (3363)
- purple (3041)
- red (3721)

KEY

a: Stem stitch, brown, 2 strands

b: Split stitch, blue, 2 strands

c: Star stitch, green, 2 strands

d: Star stitch, blue, 2 strands

e: Star stitch, purple, 2 strands

f: Star stitch, red, 2 strands

Ombré Pineapple

The best part about this pattern is using the color-changing embroidery floss. Any excuse to use that stuff is a good one. It's so fun to experiment with and see the different effects it creates. The chevron stitch is pretty easy, so this should be a fast one.

CHEVRON STITCH

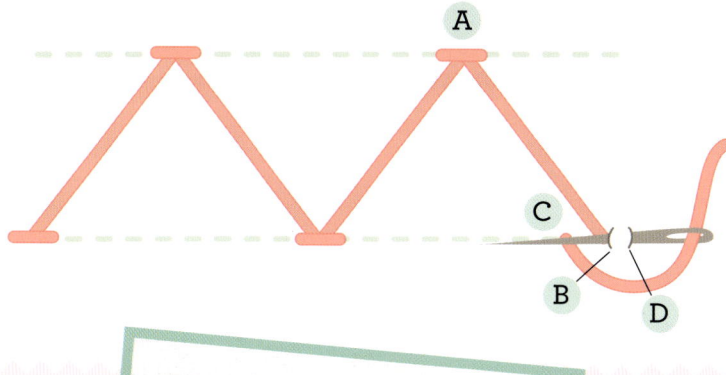

The chevron stitch is a fun design stitch that makes a zigzag with lines on the corners. Use it to add a decorative border or special touch to your embroidery project.

Bring the needle up at A and down at B. Bring the needle up at C and down at D. Do not pull tight yet. Bring the needle back up at B and pull tight. Repeat at even intervals.

YOU WILL NEED

White fabric

5-inch (12.5 cm) embroidery hoop

Template (page 107)

EMBROIDERY FLOSS

🟡 yellow (4073)

🟢 green (904)

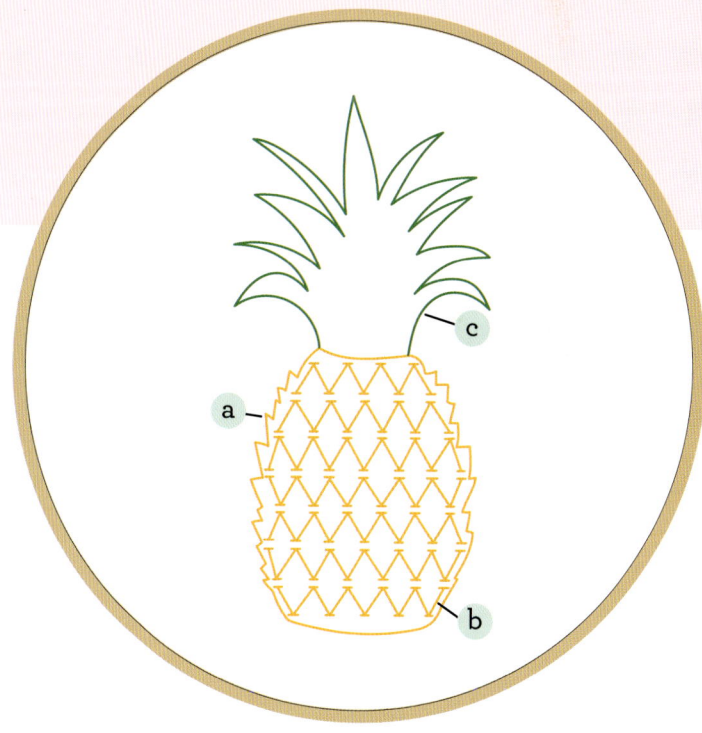

KEY

a: Back stitch, yellow, 2 strands

b: Chevron stitch, yellow, 2 strands

c: Split stitch, green, 2 strands

Lovely Lemons

The basketweave stitch creates an interesting texture for the lemons in this pattern. If you find you're having difficulty with the basketweave stitch, you can simplify it a little. Just outline the lemons in your favorite line stitch, then place the lines farther apart for your basketweave stitch.

BASKETWEAVE STITCH

This stitch is part embroidery, part weaving. It's a great way to fill an area and add a little texture at the same time. Got a pattern with a basket in it? This is the stitch you want to use.

Step 1. Bring the needle up at A and down at B to create evenly spaced, parallel stitches across the entire shape.

Step 2. Bring the needle up at C and weave over and under the stitches created in step 1. Bring the needle down at D on the other side of the shape. Repeat until the shape is filled, alternating over and under weaving with each row.

YOU WILL NEED

Light pink fabric

5-inch (12.5 cm) embroidery hoop

Template (page 107)

EMBROIDERY FLOSS

● yellow (726)

○ white (BLANC)

● green (959)

KEY

a: Basketweave stitch, yellow, 3 strands

b: Satin stitch, white, 3 strands

c: Fly stitch, green, 3 strands

d: Stem stitch, green, 3 strands

e: Stem stitch, white, 3 strands

Fly Away

I feel like I've said this about every pattern, but I love the colors on this little hot air balloon. They are so bright and summery! It's the perfect size for adding to a shirt or hat, and you could even make it smaller to use in a mini embroidery hoop for jewelry or a keychain.

THREADED RUNNING STITCH

This is a really neat stitch that creates a wavy line. You can make it with all one color or use one color for the running stitch and a different one for the threading part. You can also go back with threading in the opposite direction to make more of a chain design. This kind of threading can also be done on a back stitch for a different look (threaded back stitch). So many options!

Create a running stitch starting at A (see day 2, for running stitch on page 33). Bring the needle up at B, under the last running stitch in the line. Turn the needle so it comes out above the stitch. Slide the needle under the next stitch, coming down from the top. Keep the thread loose to retain a wavy line look. Continue to slide the needle under each of the running stitches. Alternate bringing it under from the bottom and top of each stitch.

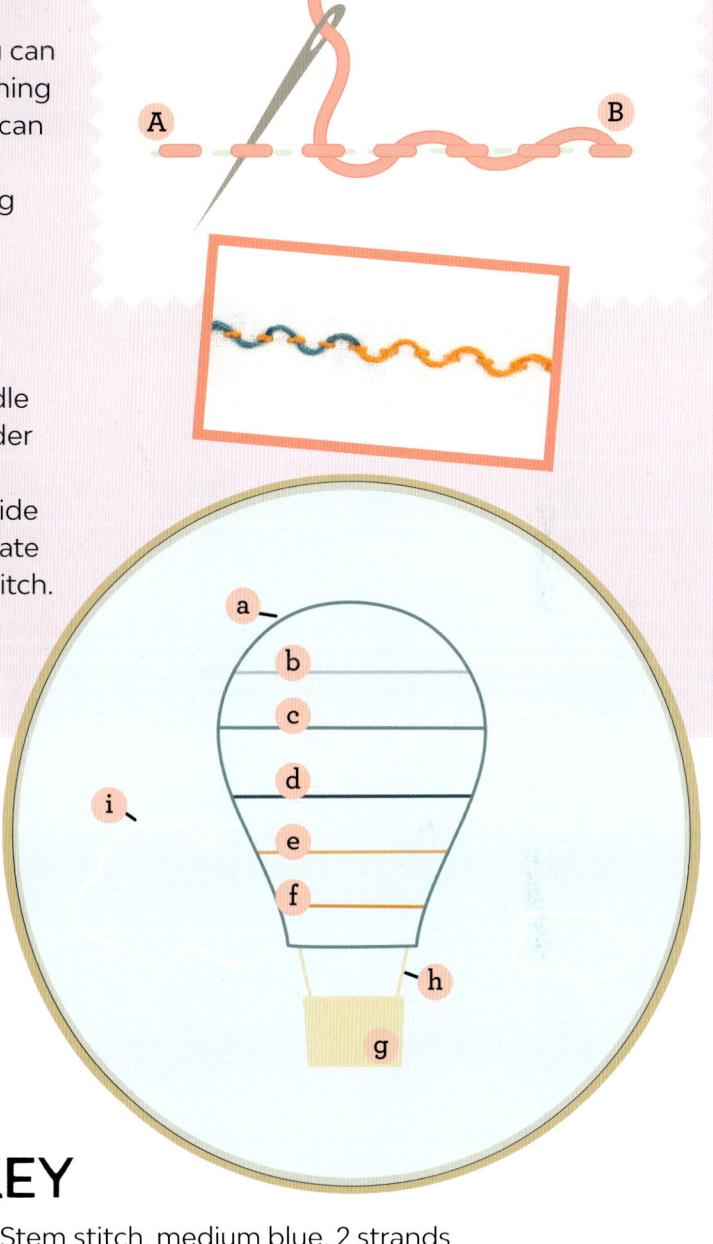

YOU WILL NEED

Light blue fabric

3-inch (7.5 cm) embroidery hoop

Template (page 119)

EMBROIDERY FLOSS

- ● medium blue (3810)
- ● light blue (519)
- ● dark blue (930)
- ● light orange (3853)
- ● dark orange (720)
- ● yellow (3047)
- ○ white (BLANC)

KEY

a: Stem stitch, medium blue, 2 strands

b: Threaded running stitch, light blue, 2 strands

c: Threaded running stitch, medium blue, 2 strands

d: Threaded running stitch, dark blue, 2 strands

e: Threaded running stitch, light orange, 2 strands

f: Threaded running stitch, dark orange, 2 strands

g: Basketweave stitch, yellow, 2 strands

h: Split stitch, yellow, 2 strands

i: Split stitch, white, 2 strands

Day at the Beach

In this pattern, you'll get to play around using the whipped back stitch in one and two colors. You'll also get to try a loose fly stitch to make the scallops on the bottom of the umbrella. Rather than having them connected like a vine, each "U" is its own shape with a small tack stitch on the bottom.

WHIPPED BACK STITCH

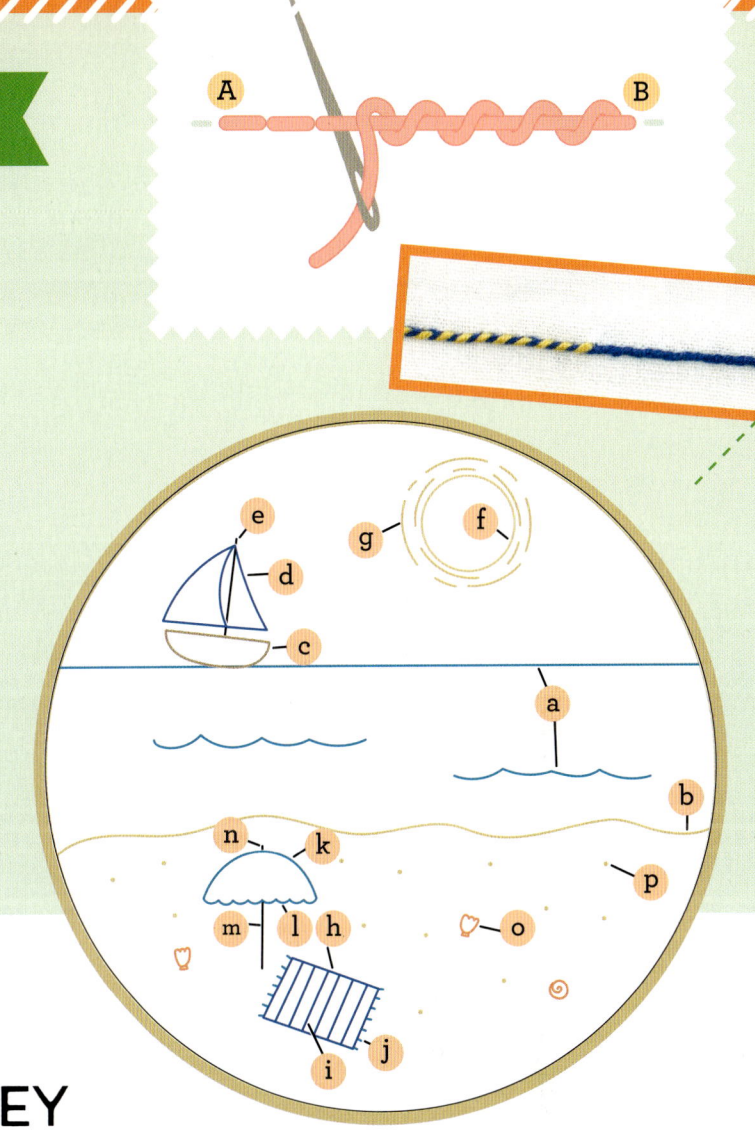

Just like with the previous stitch, you can create the whipped back stitch using a single color thread or use one color for the back stitch and a different one for the whipped part. If you use all one color, it will look like a solid line. If you use two colors, it will like the stripes on a candy cane. You can also do the same whip stitching on a running stitch for a different look (whipped running stitch).

Create a back stitch starting at A (see day 3 for back stitch on page 35). Bring the needle up at B, under the last back stitch in the line. Turn the needle so it comes out above the stitch. Slide the needle under the next stitch, coming up from the bottom. Continue to slide the needle under each of the back stitches. Come up from the bottom of the stitches every time.

YOU WILL NEED

White fabric

4-inch (10 cm) embroidery hoop

Template (page 117)

EMBROIDERY FLOSS

- blue (3810)
- yellow (676)
- brown (840)
- dark blue (824)
- black (310)
- coral (351)

KEY

a: Whipped back stitch, blue, 2 strands

b: Whipped back stitch, yellow, 2 strands

c: Split stitch, brown, 2 strands

d: Split stitch, dark blue, 2 strands

e: Stem stitch, black, 2 strands

f: Whipped back stitch, yellow, 2 strands

g: Split stitch, yellow, 2 strands

h: Back stitch, dark blue, 2 strands

i: Whipped back stitch, dark blue whipped with blue, 2 strands

j: Straight stitch, blue, 2 strands

k: Stem stitch, blue, 2 strands

l: Fly stitch (loose with no stem), blue, 2 strands

m: Back stitch, black, 2 strands

n: Straight stitch, black, 2 strands

o: Back stitch, coral, 2 strands

p: French knot, yellow, 2 strands

Wanderlust

Wouldn't you love to open up a suitcase to find this loveliness inside? I know that would make me happy. Make this pattern larger for more of a challenge, or add some French knots to the ends of each branch. To make things easier, outline the leaves and other flowers instead of filling them. Notice the ends of two branches are too long for the fly stitch, so you finish them off with a whipped back stitch.

WOVEN WHEEL STITCH

This is my favorite stitch for making flowers. You can leave them as is or add a French knot to the center. I always make them using all six strands of embroidery floss so they have a nice texture. These take a lot of embroidery floss, so I start them off using a longer piece of thread than I normally would.

Step 1. Bring the needle up at A and down at B. Make a total of five lines this way, equally spaced, ending at B.

Step 2. Bring the needle up at C, close to B. Slide the needle under and over each of the previous stitches in a circular pattern until the entire circle is filled. Don't pull too tightly or your circle will get distorted.

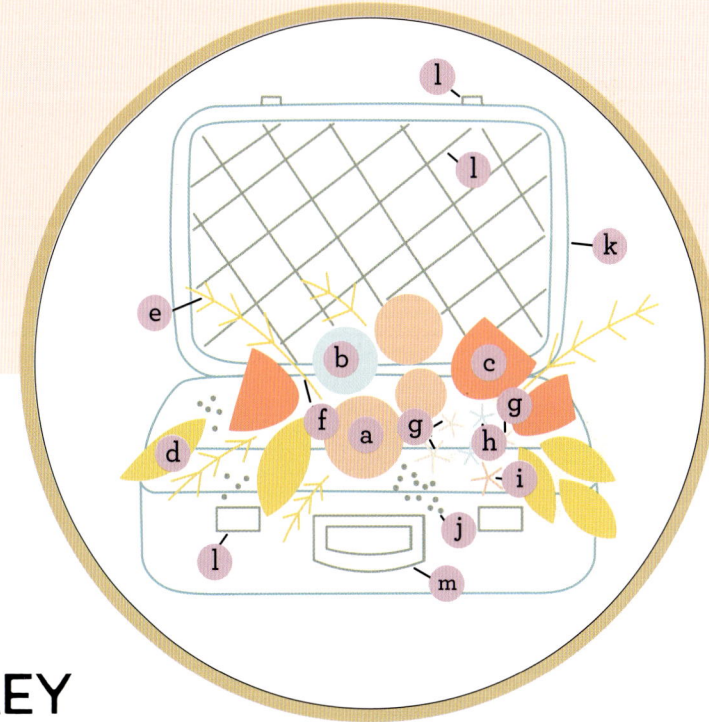

YOU WILL NEED

White fabric

4-inch (10 cm) embroidery hoop

Template (page 109)

EMBROIDERY FLOSS

- medium pink (3778)
- light blue (519)
- dark pink (351)'
- green (472)
- light pink (3779)
- gray (169)
- medium blue (3810)

KEY

a: Woven wheel stitch, medium pink, 6 strands

b: Woven wheel stitch, light blue, 6 strands

c: Satin stitch, dark pink, 3 strands

d: Fishbone stitch, green, 3 strands

e: Fly stitch, green, 2 strands

f: Whipped back stitch, green, 2 strands

g: Straight stitch, light pink, 6 strands

h: Straight stitch, light blue, 6 strands

i: Straight stitch, medium pink, 6 strands

j: French knot, gray, 2 strands

k: Split stitch, medium blue, 2 strands

l: Straight stitch, gray, 2 strands

m: Split stitch, gray, 2 strands

Cactus Flowers

The fading colors on these cactus flowers look so pretty in the looped blanket stitch. To make them a bit easier, you can create fewer rings on the flowers than the pattern calls for. The black thread for the cactus prickles will show through the white fabric, so I suggest making each one individually rather than traveling the thread across the back to the next one.

LOOPED BLANKET STITCH

This is a really pretty dimensional stitch that leaves loops on top of the fabric. I wouldn't put it on any clothing that needs to be washed, but it's really nice for decorative pieces. It makes lovely flowers when done in a circle.

Step 1. Bring the needle up at A and down at B, leaving a loop on top of the fabric. Hold the loop down for the next step if needed. Bring the needle up at C (halfway between A and B) and down at D, leaving another loop on top of the fabric. Hold the loop down for the next step if needed.

Step 2. Bring the needle up at B and down at E, leaving a loop on top of the fabric. Repeat the above steps, bringing the needle up at D for the next loop.

YOU WILL NEED

White fabric

5-inch (12.5 cm) embroidery hoop

Template (page 109)

EMBROIDERY FLOSS

- green (563)
- black (310)
- yellow (3078)
- dark pink (3778)
- medium pink (758)
- light pink (950)
- gray (169)

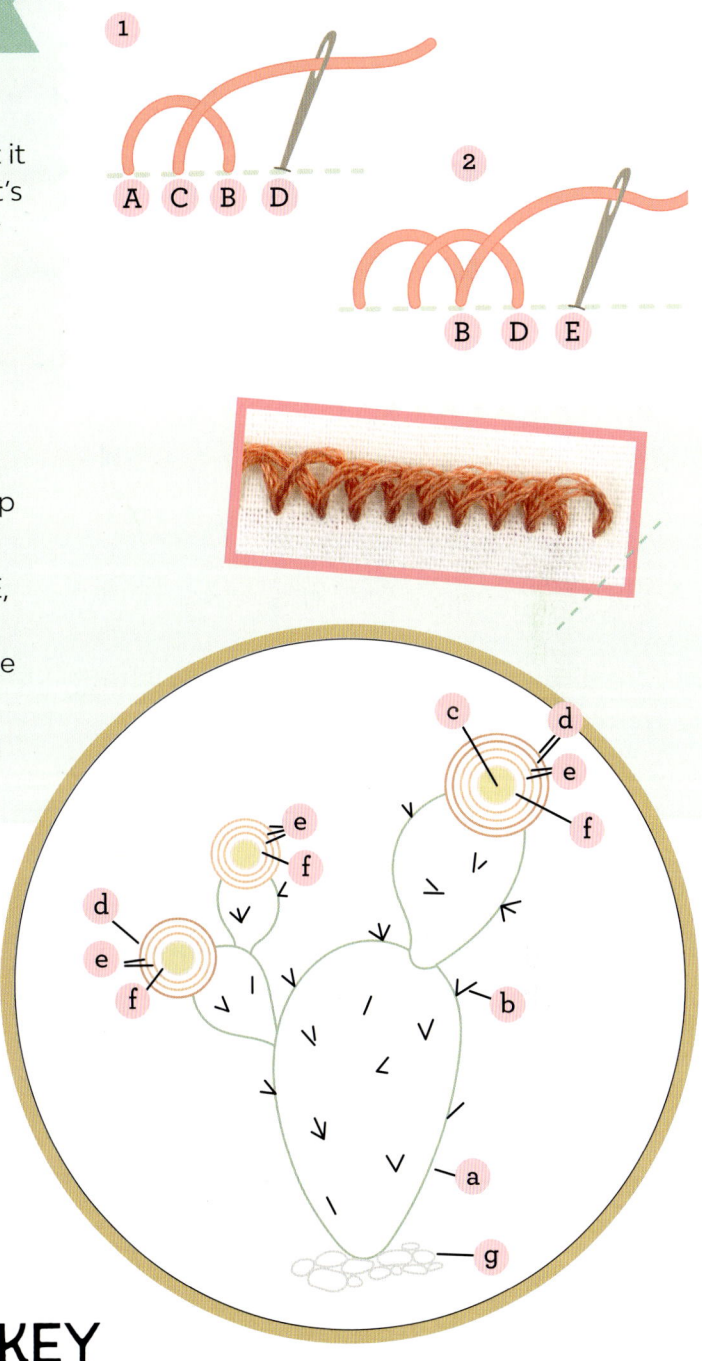

KEY

a: Whipped back stitch, green, 2 strands

b: Straight stitch, black, 2 strands

c: Satin stitch, yellow, 2 strands

d: Looped blanket stitch, dark pink, 3 strands

e: Looped blanket stitch, medium pink, 3 strands

f: Looped blanket stitch, light pink, 3 strands

g: Split stitch, gray, 2 strands

Beautiful Ballerina

I had such a hard time coming up with a pattern that wasn't another flower for the turkey stitch. I love flowers! Eventually I thought up this ballerina, and I think it's one of my favorite patterns in the book. Her features are very detailed, so you have to use a single strand of floss and tiny stitches, but it's worth it. If you have a little ballerina in your life, a set of three ballerina embroidery hoops, in different poses, would be an adorable bedroom decoration.

TURKEY STITCH

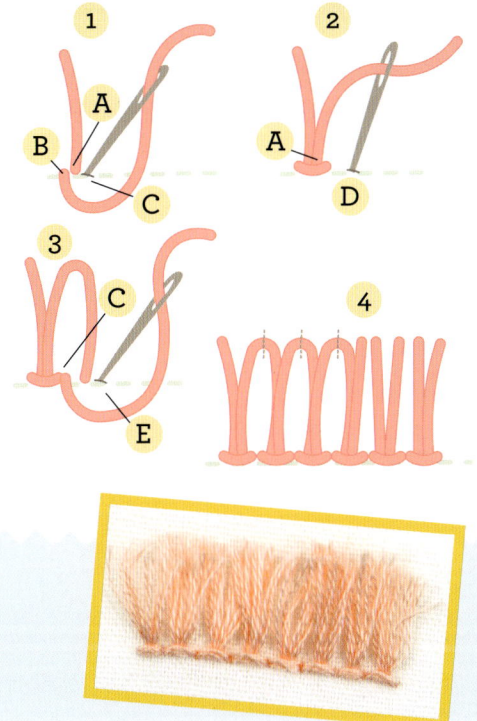

Like the looped blanket stitch, the turkey stitch is a dimensional stitch. It makes a fringe that can be turned into pretty flowers or hair. You start it by making loops that you later cut and fluff.

Step 1. For this stitch do not secure the thread in the back or tie a knot at the end of the thread. Bring the needle down at A and leave the length of thread that you'd like to have sticking out on top. Bring the needle up at B and down at C. Before pulling that all the way down, bring the needle back up at A.

Step 2. Bring the needle down at D and leave a loop the same length as the thread you left on step 1.

Step 3. Bring the needle up at C and down at E. Before pulling that all the way down, bring the needle back up at D.

Step 4. Once you finish stitching, cut open the loops at the top and separate the threads with your finger.

YOU WILL NEED

White fabric

6-inch (15 cm) embroidery hoop

Template (page 121)

EMBROIDERY FLOSS

● black (310)

● pink (3779)

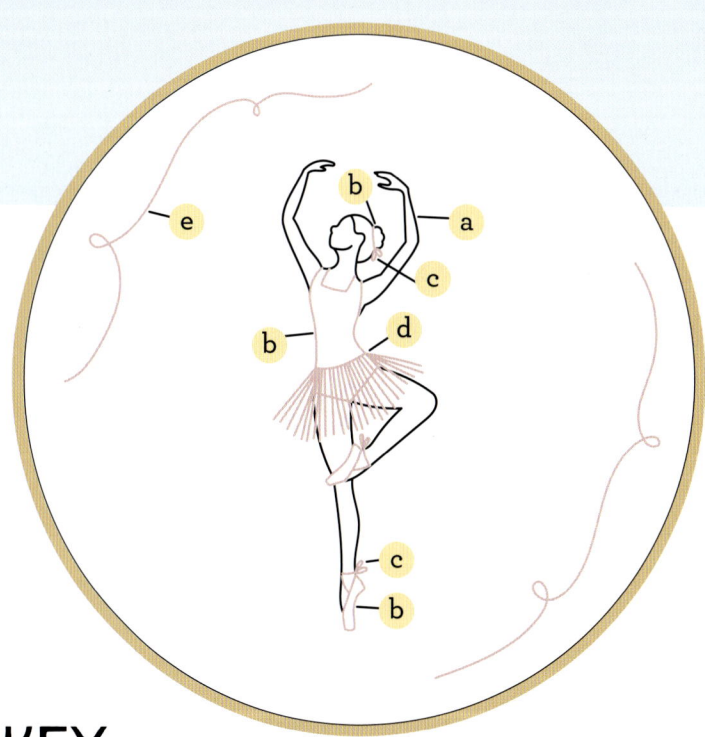

KEY

a: Split stitch, black, 1 strand

b: Split stitch, pink, 2 strands

c: Lazy daisy, pink, 2 strands

d: Turkey stitch, pink, 6 strands

e: Stem stitch, pink, 2 strands

CHAPTER 3

Next Steps

Congratulations on making it through all thirty days of stitches!
(Or maybe you skipped some, and that's completely fine too.)
Now that you have some new skills under your belt, you're ready
to move on to some new challenges. In this chapter, I'll show you
how to finish and display your hoops, give you a couple of more
involved designs to exercise your skills, and share some ideas for
taking your designs from the hoop to clothing and more.

Bonus Challenge Projects

Now that you've learned all these stitches, you're ready for a challenge! I've included two patterns that will take quite a bit more time and effort than the previous ones. They both include various stitches and lots of filling. I would have liked to include every stitch we learned in the patterns, but that wasn't very practical.

Cozy Corner

Don't you just want to curl up with a book in this cozy corner? This pattern has a lot of little details. So much so that I ran out of letters of the alphabet to use for the diagram! My favorite details are the turkey stitch tassels on the hanging planters and the large French knot flowers in the jar. The sleepy little kitty ties it all together.

White fabric

7-inch (17.5 cm) embroidery hoop

Template (page 125)

Try not to judge what your cat looks like before you've outlined it, or do the outline part first if that works better for you.

EMBROIDERY FLOSS

- brown (898)
- light brown (840)
- orange (676)
- blue (930)
- light blue (3811)
- coral (356)

- yellow (726)
- pink (3713)
- purple (3807)
- mint (3817)
- dark gray (3799)
- tan (3864)

- dark green (319)
- off-white (543)
- green (904)
- peach (3771)

KEY

a: Stem stitch, brown, 3 strands

b: Straight stitch, brown, 3 strands

c: Satin stitch, light brown, 2 strands

d: Brick stitch, light brown, 2 strands

e: Satin stitch, orange, 2 strands

f: Satin stitch, blue, 2 strands

g: Satin stitch, light blue, 2 strands

h: Satin stitch, coral, 2 strands

i: Satin stitch, yellow, 2 strands

j: Satin stitch, pink, 2 strands

k: Satin stitch, purple, 2 strands

l: Satin stitch, mint, 2 strands

m: Satin stitch, dark gray, 2 strands

n: Long and short stitch, tan, 1 strand

o: Back stitch, brown, 1 strand

p: Straight stitch, dark gray, 2 strands

q: Stem stitch, dark gray, 2 stands

r: Split stitch, light brown, 3 strands

s: Straight stitch, dark green, 2 strands

t: French knot, off-white, 6 strands

u: Fishbone stitch, green, 2 strands

v: Split stitch, green, 2 strands

w: Long and short stitch, peach, 1 strand

x: Satin stitch, coral, 2 strands

y: Long and short stitch, coral, 2 strands

z: Fill couching stitch, green, 2 strands

1: Back stitch, light brown, 3 strands

2: Straight stitch, light brown, 3 strands

3: Long and short stitch, dark gray, 1 strand

4: Palestrina stitch, off-white, 2 strands

5: Straight stitch, off-white, 2 strands

6: Turkey stitch, off-white, 3 strands

7: Whipped back stitch, off-white, 2 strands

8: Lazy daisy stitch, green, 2 strands

9: Split stitch, green, 1 strand

10: Long and short stitch, light brown, 1 strand

11: French knot, dark green, 2 strands

12: Whipped back stitch, off-white whipped with peach, 2 strands

13: Running stitch, coral, 2 strands

14: Back stitch, off-white, 2 strands

15: Herringbone stitch, peach, 1 strand

Enchanted Evening

This lovely scene is sure to test your skills with lots of filling and varied stitches. Notice the direction in which each filling stitch on the mushrooms goes in the photos. That's important to get them to look right. You'll also notice that one of the lines on the star stitch is left out, which makes them less bulky.

YOU WILL NEED

teal fabric

6-inch (15 cm) embroidery hoop

Template (page 123)

EMBROIDERY FLOSS

- red (919)
- white (BLANC)
- off-white (739)
- pink (352)
- light pink (353)
- dark brown (898)
- brown (840)
- blue (932)
- black (310)
- green (3053)

KEY

a: Long and short stitch, red, 2 strands

b: Fill with chain stitch in circles, white, 2 strands

c: Brick stitch, off-white, 3 strands

d: Satin stitch, pink, 2 strands

e: Satin stitch, pink, 3 strands

f: Satin stitch, light pink, 2 strands

g: Long and short stitch, light pink, 2 strands

h: Satin stitch, off-white, 2 strands

i: Split stitch, dark brown, 2 strands

j: Fill with split stitch, brown, 2 strands

k: Back stitch, off-white, 2 strands

l: French knot, off-white, 2 strands

m: Buttonhole stitch, blue, 2 strands

n: Satin stitch, black, 2 strands

o: Back stitch, black, 2 strands

p: Straight stitch, black, 2 strands

q: Basketweave stitch, white, 3 strands

r: Star stitch, white, 2 strands

s: Colonial knot, white, 2 strands

t: Stem stitch, green, 2 strands

u: Fishbone stitch, green, 2 strands

v: Split stitch, brown, 2 strands

Finishing Your Hoops

YOU WILL NEED

Embroidery hoop

Embroidery floss

Felt (a wool/rayon blend works best)

Scissors

Pinking shears (optional)

Embroidery needle

I like to frame the projects I love most in embroidery hoops. I have a whole wall of embroidery hoop art in my craft room, and I love looking at it. Here's how I like to frame my finished embroidery designs.

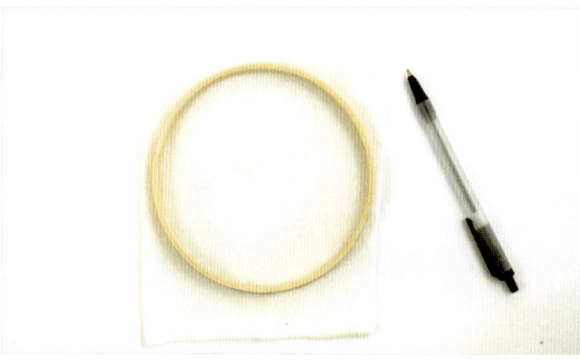

Step 1. Trace the outside of the inner ring of the embroidery hoop onto a piece of felt and cut it out.

Step 2. Cut the excess fabric around the hoop, leaving about an inch (2.5 cm). I use pinking shears to stop the fabric from fraying, but that's optional.

Step 3. Cut a piece of embroidery floss long enough to go around the hoop plus a few inches. Separate out three strands and thread them on a needle. Starting at the top, stitch around the excess fabric on the back of the hoop with a long running stitch (see page 33). Leave a tail of thread a couple inches (5 cm) long.

Step 4. Once you've stitched around the entire hoop, pull both tails of the thread, like a drawstring bag. Tie a double knot in the top and trim off the excess thread.

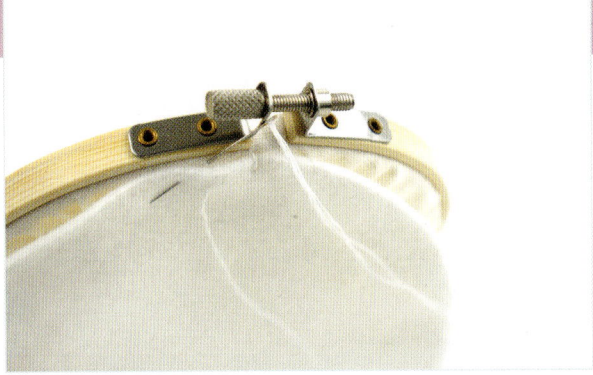

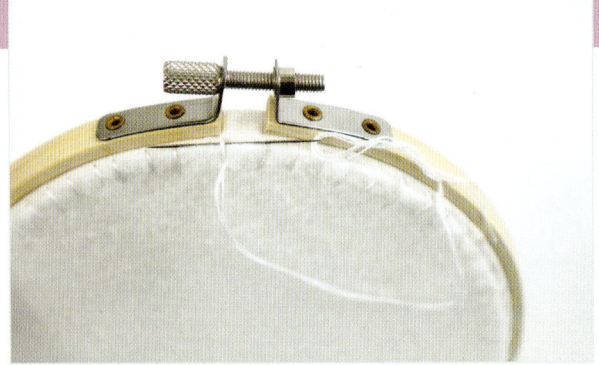

Step 5. Cut a piece of floss long enough to go around the hoop two and a half times. Thread three strands on a needle. Place the circle of felt on the back of the hoop and attach the felt to the excess fabric with a whip stitch. (To sew a whip stitch, bring your needle up through the back of the felt, bring it over the edge of the felt, push your needle up and down through the excess embroidery fabric, then bring it back through the back of the felt at an angle.)

Step 6. When you've stitched around the entire felt circle, bring the needle back up where you started, slide it under a previous stitch, and tie a double knot. Push the needle through some of the embroidery fabric on the back.

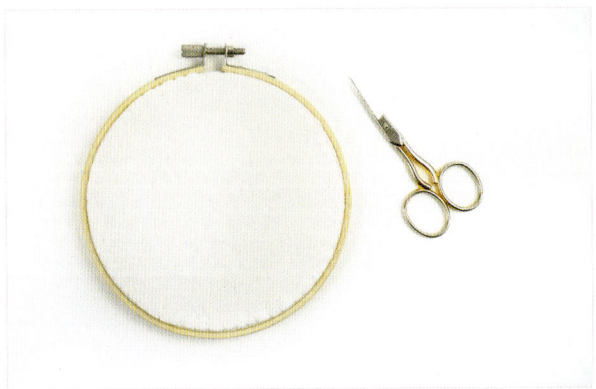

Step 7. Trim off the excess thread. You now have a neat, finished backing that hides all the messy threads.

Ideas for Using Embroidery

Framing embroidery and hanging it on the wall is fun and all, but what about stitching on practical things? You can stitch on almost anything made of fabric. Experiment with things like T-shirts, jeans, tote bags, hats, and even shoes. Here are just a few practical ways to use your new embroidery skills.

MINIATURE EMBROIDERY PENDANT

This is such a fun way to show off little bits of embroidery. Use a copier to reduce the size of the simpler patterns to make them into jewelry or keychains. Search for jewelry blanks or mini embroidery hoops like this one that are meant for small embroidery projects. I reduced the "Fly Away" pattern from this book by 50 percent and it fit perfectly in this little hoop. You might need to change the number of strands or take out some of the details. I also simplified the colors.

CUSTOM TOTE BAG

Just like when embroidering a T-shirt, I use water-soluble stabilizer to transfer the pattern. The fabric is usually too thick to see through for tracing, and the stabilizer makes it so easy. Tote bags aren't usually stretchy though, so you don't have to worry as much about the hoop stretching it out. Any of the patterns in this book could work for a tote, but I think the ballerina is perfect for taking to ballet class. Show off some extra skills by adding your little ballerina's name too.

EMBELLISHED T-SHIRT

When you're proud of your work and want to show it off to the world, why not add it to a T-shirt? You'll just need to follow a few extra tips.

Stabilizer

Since T-shirt fabric is stretchy, you'll need to use a stabilizer to keep it from stretching while you stitch. Luckily the water-soluble Sulky Fabri-Solvy stabilizer I showed you how to use for transferring a pattern is used for just this purpose. Follow the same instructions for transferring a pattern (see page 23), but make sure to cut the stabilizer larger than the embroidery hoop you're using.

The Hoop

Be careful not to stretch the T-shirt fabric when putting it in your hoop. You want it to be tight, but let the stabilizer do its job. No tugging on the fabric, or your design will distort.

Putting the area you want to embroider in a hoop and stabilizing the fabric will make it easier to stitch.

Stitch Length

You want to use very short stitches for clothing items. This is especially true for stretchy T-shirts. For this pattern I changed the straight stitch to a couching stitch. You also want to avoid any dimensional stitches, such as woven wheels, looped blanket stitches, and turkey stitches, on clothing.

Backing

This is optional, but I like to add an iron-on backing to my clothing items once they're complete. It makes the shirt more comfortable to wear and protects the stitches. My favorite product for this is Sulky Tender Touch.

Traceable Templates

Use these black-and-white templates to trace the designs on your fabric. See page 23 for instructions. They are printed at the same size I used them, but you can copy them to make them easier to transfer.

You can also scan the QR code below to download the templates.

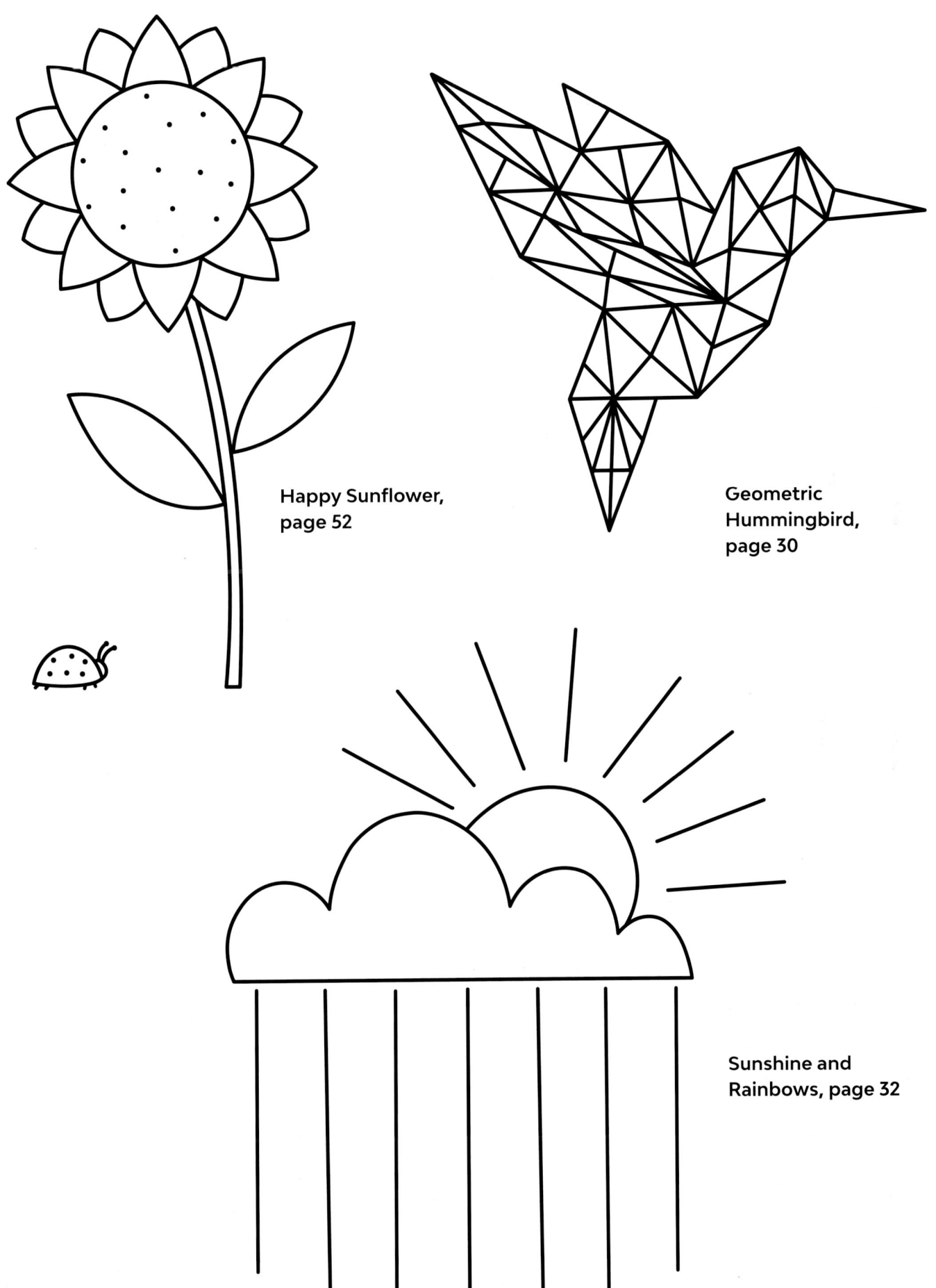

Happy Sunflower,
page 52

Geometric
Hummingbird,
page 30

Sunshine and
Rainbows, page 32

Bold Butterfly, page 60

Just Add Sprinkles, page 56

Illuminate, page 42

**Light as a Feather,
page 50**

Love Letter, page 34

Ombré Pineapple, page 76

Hourglass, page 74

Lovely Lemons,
page 78

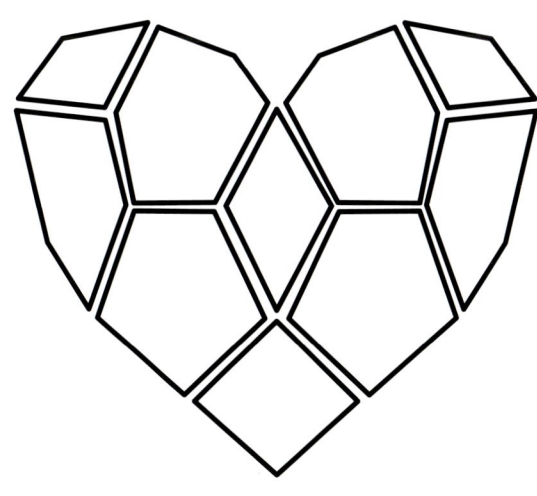

Geometric Heart, page 46

Wanderlust, page 84

Cactus Flower, page 86

Daisy Bouquet, page 38

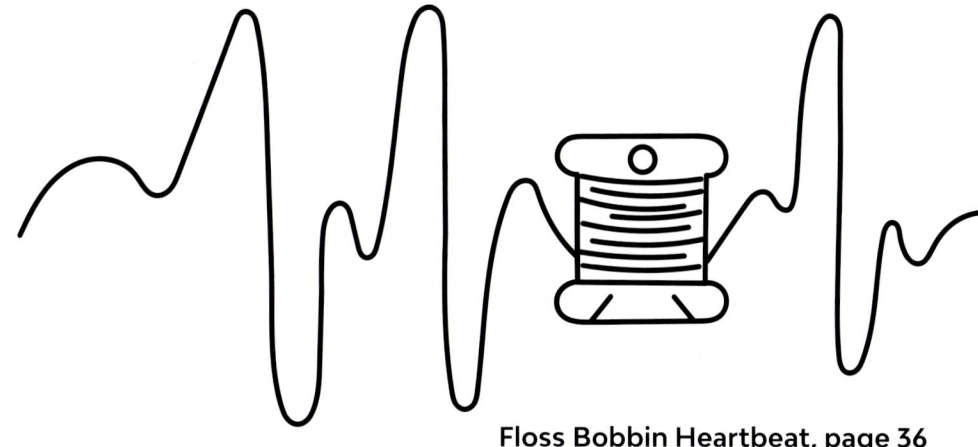

Floss Bobbin Heartbeat, page 36

Swirly Snail, page 40

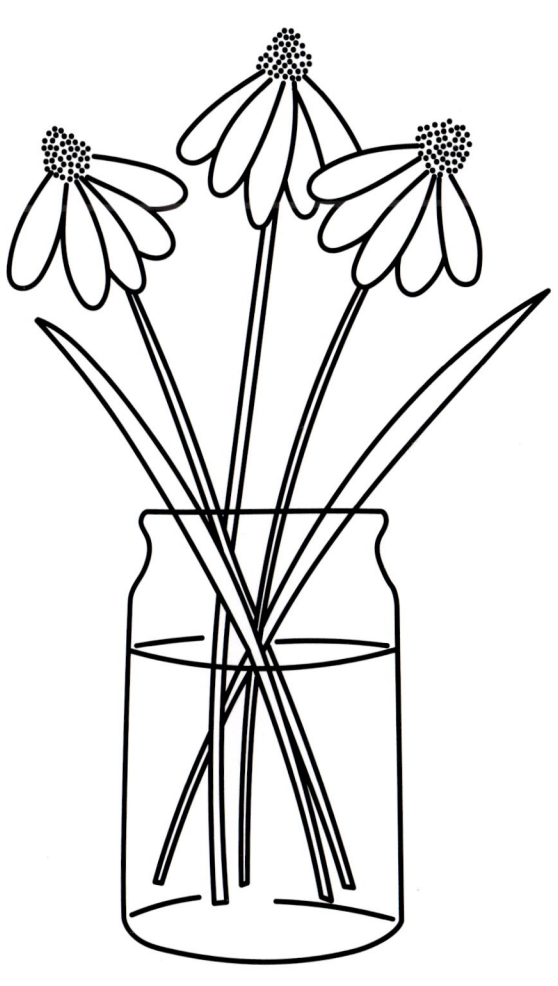

Freshly Picked, page 54

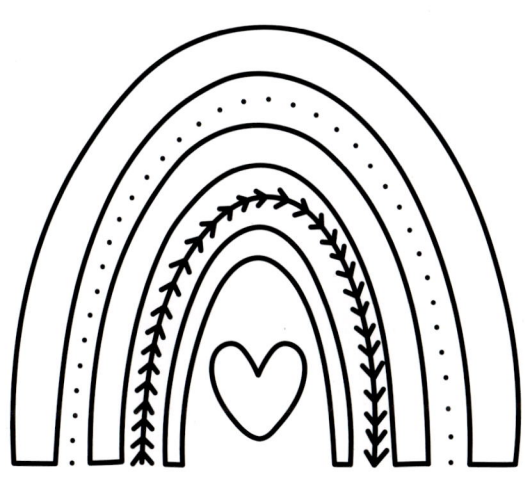

Boho Rainbow, page 68

Koi Pond, page 64

In the Garden, page 62

Dandelion Wishes, page 58

Birdseed, page 72

Busy Bee Garden, page 70

Day at the Beach, page 82

Windy Day, page 66

Fly Away, page 80

Dragonfly, page 48

Beautiful Ballerina, page 88

Happy Houseplant, page 44

Enchanted Evening, page 96

Cozy Corner, page 94

Index

Automatic needle threaders, 19

Back stitch, 28
   Busy Bee Garden project using, 70–71
   Cozy Corner project using, 93–95
   Daisy Bouquet project using, 39
   Day at the Beach project using, 82–83
   Enchanted Evening project using, 96–97
   explained, 35
   Floss Bobbin Heartbeat project using, 37
   Freshly Picked project using, 54–55
   In the Garden project using, 62–63
   Happy Sunflower project using, 52–53
   Illuminate project using, 42–43
   Just Add Sprinkles project using, 56–57
   Light as a Feather project using, 50–51
   Love Letter project using, 34–35
   Ombré Pineapple, 76–77
   Swirly Snail project using, 40–41
   Windy Day project using, 66–67
Basketweave stitch, 29
   Enchanted Evening project using, 96–97
   explained, 79
   Fly Away project using, 80–81
   Lovely Lemons project using, 78–79
Beautiful Ballerina, 11, 88–89, 121
Birdseed, 10, 72–73, 115
Black fabric, embroidery projects using, 60–61
Blow-dryer, 23
Boho Rainbow, 10, 68–69, 111
Bold Butterfly, 10, 60–61, 105
Brick stitch, 29
   Boho Rainbow project using, 68–69
   Cozy Corner project using, 93–95
   Enchanted Evening project using, 96–97
   explained, 69
Bullion knot, 29
   explained, 57
   Just Add Sprinkles project using, 56–57
Bullion needle, 18
Busy Bee Garden, 10, 70–71, 117
Buttonhole stitch, 29
   Busy Bee Garden project using, 70–71
   Enchanted Evening project using, 96–97
   explained, 71

Cactus Flowers, 11, 86–87, 109
Chain stitch, 28
   Boho Rainbow project using, 68–69
   Enchanted Evening project using, 96–97

explained, 41
   Swirly Snail project using, 40–41
Chevron stitch, 29, 76–77
Colonial knot, 29
   Enchanted Evening project using, 96–97
   explained, 55
   Freshly Picked project using, 54–55
Colored fabric, embroidery projects using, 40–41, 50–51, 58–59, 68–71, 78–81, 96–97
Cotton fabric, 17
Couching stitch, 28
   Cozy Corner project using, 93–95
   explained, 51
   Light as a Feather project using, 50–51
Cozy Corner, 93–95, 125
Curves, stitching with, 32, 34, 43

Daisy Bouquet, 8, 38–39, 109
Dandelion Wishes, 9, 58–59, 115
Dark fabric. See also Colored fabric, embroidery projects using
   embroidery projects using, 58–61
   transferring pattern onto, 24
Day at the Beach, 11, 82–83, 117
DMC brand embroidery floss, 17
Dragonfly, 9, 48–49, 121

Embroidery floss/threads, 17
   not showing through on other side of fabric, 22
   number of strands to use, 20
   securing, 21
   separating, 20
Embroidery hoops, 18
   framing your embroidery projects in, 98–99
   putting your fabric in, 25
Embroidery needles, 18
Enchanted Evening, 96–97, 123
Essex Linen, 17

Fabric, 17. See also Colored fabric, embroidery projects using
   putting in an embroidery hoop, 25
   transferring patterns on to dark or patterned, 24
   transferring patterns to the, 23
Feather stitch, 29, 64–65
Felt, framing your embroidery projects using, 98–99
Fishbone stitch, 28
   Cozy Corner project using, 93–95
   Enchanted Evening project using, 96–97
   explained, 45

Happy Houseplant project using, 44–45
   Wanderlust project using, 84–85
Floss Bobbin Heartbeat, 8, 36–37, 111
Fly Away, 11, 80–81, 119
Fly stitch, 29
   Boho Rainbow project using, 68–69
   Day at the Beach project using, 82–83
   explained, 63
   In the Garden project using, 62–63
   Lovely Lemons project using, 78–79
   Wanderlust project using, 84–85
Framing embroidery designs, 98–99
French knot, 28
   Boho Rainbow project using, 68–69
   Busy Bee Garden project using, 70–71
   Cozy Corner project using, 93–95
   Day at the Beach project using, 82–83
   Enchanted Evening project using, 96–97
   explained, 52–53
   Happy Sunflower project using, 52–53
   Wanderlust project using, 84–85
Freshly Picked, 9, 54–55, 111
FriXion pen, 19, 23, 24

Geometric Heart, 9, 46–47, 109
Geometric Hummingbird, 8, 30–31, 103

Happy Houseplant, 9, 44–45, 123
Happy Sunflower, 9, 52–53, 103
Herringbone stitch, 29
   Cozy Corner project using, 93–95
   explained, 67
   Windy Day project using, 66–67
Hourglass, 10, 74–75, 107

Illuminate, 9, 42–43, 105
In the Garden, 10, 62–63, 113

Just Add Sprinkles, 9, 56–57, 105

Knots, 21. See also Bullion knot; Colonial knot; French knot
Koi Pond, 10, 64–65, 113

Lazy daisy stitch, 28
   Beautiful Ballerina project using, 88–89
   Busy Bee Garden project using, 70–71
   Cozy Corner project using, 93–95
   Daisy Bouquet project using, 38–39
   explained, 39
   In the Garden project using, 62–63
   Illuminate project using, 42–43
Light as a Feather, 9, 50–51, 105
Light table, 19
Linen/cotton blend fabric, 17

Long and short stitch, 28
  Cozy Corner project using, 93–95
  Dragonfly project using, 48–49
  Enchanted Evening project using,
    96–97
  explained, 49
Looped blanket stitch, 29, 86–87
Love Letter, 8, 34–35, 107
Lovely Lemons, 11, 78–79, 107

Magnetic needle minder, 18
Milliner's needle, 18

Natural linen-colored fabric, embroi-
    dery project using, 38–39, 72–73
Needle sizes, 18
Needle threader, 19

Ombré Pineapple, 10, 76–77, 107

Palestrina stitch, 29
  Bold Butterfly project using, 60–61
  Cozy Corner project using, 93–95
  explained, 61
Patterned fabric, transferring patterns
    onto, 24
Pendant, miniature embroidery, 100
Pistil stitch, 29
  Bold Butterfly project using, 60–61
  Dandelion Wishes project using,
    58–59
  explained, 59

Running stitch, 28
  Busy Bee Garden project using, 70–71
  Cozy Corner project using, 93–95
  explained, 33
  Fly Away project using, 80–81
  Love Letter project using, 34–35
  Sunshine and Rainbows project
    using, 32–33

Satin stitch, 28
  Birdseed project using, 72–73
  Boho Rainbow project using, 68–69
  Bold Butterfly project using, 60–61
  Busy Bee Garden project using, 70–71
  Cactus Flowers project using, 86–87
  Cozy Corner project using, 93–95
  Enchanted Evening project using,
    96–97
  explained, 47
  Freshly Picked project using, 54–55
  In the Garden project using, 62–63
  Geometric Heart project using, 46–47
  Just Add Sprinkles project using,
    56–57
  Koi Pond project using, 64–65
  Lovely Lemons project using, 78–79
  Wanderlust project using, 84–85
  Windy Day project using, 66–67
Scissors, 19
Seed stitch, 29, 72–73

Split stitch, 28
  Beautiful Ballerina project using,
    88–89
  Birdseed project using, 72–73
  Bold Butterfly project using, 60–61
  Busy Bee Garden project using, 70–71
  Cactus Flowers project using, 86–87
  Cozy Corner project using, 93–95
  Daisy Bouquet project using, 39
  Day at the Beach project using, 82–83
  Dragonfly project using, 48–49
  Enchanted Evening project using,
    96–97
  explained, 37
  Floss Bobbin Heartbeat project using,
    36–37
  Fly Away project using, 80–81
  Freshly Picked project using, 54–55
  In the Garden project using, 62–63
  Happy Houseplant project using,
    44–45
  Happy Sunflower project using, 52–53
  Hourglass project using, 74–75
  Illuminate project using, 42–43
  Just Add Sprinkles project using,
    56–57
  Koi Pond project using, 64–65
  Ombré Pineapple, 76–77
  Swirly Snail project using, 40–41
  Wanderlust project using, 84–85
  Windy Day project using, 66–67
Stabilizer, 24
Star stitch, 29
  Enchanted Evening project using,
    96–97
  explained, 75
  Hourglass project using, 74–75
Stem stitch, 28
  Beautiful Ballerina project using,
    88–89
  Birdseed project using, 72–73
  Bold Butterfly project using, 60–61
  Busy Bee Garden project using, 70–71
  Cozy Corner project using, 93–95
  Dandelion Wishes project using,
    58–59
  Day at the Beach project using, 82–83
  Enchanted Evening project using,
    96–97
  explained, 43
  Fly Away project using, 80–81
  Happy Sunflower project using, 52–53
  Hourglass project using, 74–75
  Illuminate project using, 42–43
  Just Add Sprinkles project using,
    56–57
  Koi Pond project using, 64–65
  Lovely Lemons project using, 78–79
  Swirly Snail project using, 40–41
  Windy Day project using, 66–67
Stitches. See also specific stitches
  glossary of, 28–29
  securing the floss for, 21
Straight stitch, 28
  Birdseed project using, 72–73

Cactus Flowers project using, 86–87
  Cozy Corner project using, 93–95
  Daisy Bouquet project using, 39
  Day at the Beach project using, 82–83
  Enchanted Evening project using,
    96–97
  explained, 31
  In the Garden project using, 62–63
  Geometric Hummingbird project
    using, 30–31
  Happy Houseplant project using,
    44–45
  Happy Sunflower project using, 52–53
  Koi Pond project using, 64–65
  Love Letter project using, 34–35
  Wanderlust project using, 84–85
Sulky Fabri-Solvy stabilizer, 19, 24
Sunshine and Rainbows, 8, 32–33, 103
Supplies, 16–19
Swirly Snail, 8, 40–41, 111

T-shirt, embellished, 101
Templates, 103–125
Threaded running stitch, 29, 80–81
Tote bag, 100
Transferring an embroidery pattern, 19,
    23
Traveling threads, 22
Turkey stitch, 29
  Beautiful Ballerina project using,
    88–89
  Cozy Corner project using, 93–95
  explained, 89

Wanderlust, 11, 84–85, 109
Water-soluble stabilizer, 19, 100, 101
Whipped back stitch, 29
  Cactus Flowers project using, 86–87
  Cozy Corner project using, 93–95
  Day at the Beach project using, 82–83
  explained, 83
  Wanderlust project using, 84–85
White fabric, embroidery projects
    using, 30–37, 42–49, 52–57, 62–67,
    74–77, 82–89, 93–95
Windy Day, 10, 66–67, 119
Woven wheel stitch, 29, 84–85

About the Author

Jessica Anderson is an avid crafter and embroidery artist. She shares creative ideas on her blog, Cutesy Crafts, and has taught thousands of people to embroider through her YouTube channel. Her crafts have also been published in several magazines, including *Better Homes & Gardens*, *Country Woman*, *Homespun*, and *Mollie Makes*. She lives in Sacramento, California, with her husband and four children.